Its Beauty For Ashes

HEALING IN THE WAKE OF BROKENNESS

Carmen Ramos

Copyright © 2024 by Carmen Ramos

All rights reserved.

No portion of this book may be reproduced in any form without written permission from the publisher or author, except as permitted by U.S. copyright law.

This publication is designed to provide accurate and authoritative information in regard to the subject matter covered. It is sold with the understanding that neither the author nor the publisher is engaged in rendering legal, investment, accounting or other professional services. While the publisher and author have used their best efforts in preparing this book, they make no representations or warranties with respect to the accuracy or completeness of the contents of this book and specifically disclaim any implied warranties of merchantability or fitness for a particular purpose. No warranty may be created or extended by sales representatives or written sales materials. The advice and strategies contained herein may not be suitable for your situation. You should consult with a professional when appropriate. Neither the publisher nor the author shall be liable for any loss of profit or any other commercial damages, including but not limited to special, incidental, consequential, personal, or other damages.

Book Cover by Corey Brooks

Photography by Brendy_Photography

First Edition 2024

Scripture quotations noted KJV are from The Holy Bible: King James Version. (2011) Hendrickson. (Original work published 1611)

Scripture quotations marked NKJV are from the NEW KING JAMES VERSION. Copyright ©1979,1980,1982, Thomas Nelson, Inc. Publishers

Scripture quotations noted ESV are from the English Standard Version Bible. (2001)

Scripture quotations marked NIV are from the Holy Bible, New International Version®, NIV® Copyright ©1973, 1978, 1984, 2011 by Biblica, Inc.® Used by permission. All rights reserved worldwide.

Contents

Acknowledgments	V
Dedication	VII
Preface	VIII
Introduction	X
Section 1	
1. What Was it Really Like?	2
2. The Rude Awakening	15
3. Church, Jesus, Home & Compromise	20
Section 2	
4. He Made Himself Known	28
5. The Beginning of the End	43
6. Misunderstood Rebellion	48
7. The Attempts	63

Section 3

8. The Breakup — 72

9. The Aftermath — 77

10. Down to the Wire — 90

Section 4

11. Our Journey — 98

12. Running From God — 108

13. Confirmed — 115

14. A Dark Beginning — 131

Section 5

15. Moving On — 140

16. Ava — 148

17. Turbulence — 165

18. Pride Comes Before The Fall — 179

19. The Meeting With Jesus — 189

Section 6

20. The Transition — 202

21. Mom... We Will Keep Trying — 220

22. Dad... It's Goodbye for Now, but Not Forever — 230

23. Its Beauty for Ashes — 236

Acknowledgments

I must start by giving a huge shout-out to my incredible husband, Alex. You have been my rock throughout this entire journey. I can't thank you enough for believing in me and constantly pushing me to believe in myself. You have an extraordinary gift to bring out the best in others, and you did this with me, too. Doing life with you is an absolute delight; it never feels like a chore. I'm genuinely grateful for your strong leadership and your pure heart. Thank you for always keeping God at the forefront. It's you and me baby against the world! Our love was worth waiting for.

To my precious kiddos, you two are the light of my life. Your smiles, hugs, and presence in my life are constant reminders of God's faithfulness. I wouldn't be the person I am today if God hadn't blessed me with both of you. My love for you knows no bounds. You've given my life an entirely new and meaningful purpose.

I also want to express my heartfelt thanks to my pastors. Your support and encouragement mean the world to me. You've always been there, cheering me on and offering your time and resources. Thank you for holding me accountable, helping me grow, and pushing me to break through every ceiling in my life. Thank you for your commitment to remain pure before the Lord. Thank you for choosing to love the Lord beyond your desires. Thank you for leading through example.

To my dear friend and soul sister, Jessica, my heart swells with gratitude. Your presence in my life is an incredible blessing. You've stood by me through thick and thin, offering emotional and spiritual support during all the twists and turns of life. You've been my haven and even played the role of an earthly and spiritual mother when I needed it most. A wise person once said to me, "If you have even just one friend, you are blessed." And I am blessed. As we always say, "*It's wepa time all the time, and come what may, we will dance in the rain!*"

As I prepare to share my personal experiences, I want to acknowledge that some were tough to revisit, while others filled me with immense gratitude. Whether they involved difficult transitions, betrayals, or hardships, each experience has left its mark on me and has shaped me into the person I've become. I'm truly grateful for all of them, and I firmly believe that nothing in life is wasted because God has a way of making all things beautiful.

"And we know that in all things, God works for the good of those who love him, who have been called according to his purpose."
Romans 8:28 (NIV)

Dedication

I dedicate this book to my loving husband and children. Although you all are not the result of my deliverance and freedom, each of you is a blessing and my prized possession. I'm so thankful that God gave me the courage to give up what I thought was life because if I had not, I would have missed out on this beautiful thing we get to experience called life.

Preface

With all the words I've gathered to express my gratitude towards Jesus, my Lord, and Savior, my words still fall short of describing all He has done for me. There aren't enough pages to fill or definitions that can capture His greatness and goodness. Nothing I have laid down or given up could compare to that grand exchange of life He gave me in return. I've been graced and blessed with the gift to lead His children into healing, deliverance, and freedom through prophetic worship. Through this book, I aim to lead those I may never meet face-to-face into healing, deliverance, and freedom with the word of my testimony through the power of the Holy Spirit.

In sharing my story, I purposely confront things that some may not have the courage to face. Why? Because I must! I am indebted to my generation and the next, whom I will pass the baton to. I believe my story will empower young and old from all walks of life to believe that their failures, downfalls, and trials are not the end of them.

I know that our Heavenly Father desires that all may know there is a way out of darkness. I know He wants His children, even those who do not yet recognize themselves as His, to see He is good! My story, my life, is a testament to the good news! His kindness is what led me to repentance. His goodness, which I do not deserve, led me to the cross. He is the lover of my soul. He is my beautiful Jesus.

"For I have taken and seen that the Lord is good!
Psalm 34:8

Introduction

To all of those who are on a quest to discover their identity in Christ, this book is for you. I pray that you see your self as He sees you. Fearfully and wonderfully made! As you read my story and find God's fingerprints through it from start to finish, I pray that you understand and accept that your past, struggles, or doubts do not define you. You are defined by the One who created you. You are more than a conqueror through Christ Jesus! May you find the strength to forgive and the willpower to let go and love well. Your purpose and your destiny is victory.

Section 1

Chapter One

What Was it Really Like?

I grew up in a home where, most of the time, I was anxious. Joy felt rare. The kind of joy I experienced growing up is what I liked to call a "controlled joy." One that came with a barometer. When the joy barometer marked "out of control," that meant the joke struck a nerve. Dad was triggered and in a bad mood. Then came the unspoken rule: "tread lightly." I didn't know how to tread lightly; more so what tread lightly even meant. I just had hoped that Dad's anger would blow over quickly.

I think I discovered what anxiety and stress were way before I understood what anxiety and stress really were, which leads me to explain why. I believed that joy and pain were the worst combination of emotions and that there was no hopeful or healthy way to navigate both. Growing up in a Puerto Rican household made thoughts like this a truth. Along with many cultural superstitions and bad theologies that were knitted into this thought process and were passed down. I heard many superstitions and theories through sayings we seemed to live by. For example, one Spanish saying says, "*Dime con quién tú andas, y te diré quién tú eres.*" This means tell me who is in your circle, and I'll be able to tell what kind of person you are. There was another one that we seemed to live out, even if it was subconsciously. This one says, "*El que ría mucho termina llorando.*" This translates to, if you laugh too much, you'll end up crying. So when joy arrived, and nothing bad followed, I felt a sense of relief, like I had dodged a bullet. That meant no arguments, bad days at school, or bullying—I had managed to escape them all.

When joy graced us with its presence, a part of me became apprehensive, fearing its warmth, wondering what would come next. My father seemed to be more attached to these superstitions than my mother was since he was the one who would say them more. As a child, I assumed it dictated his mood and made him careful about enjoying life because he was so stern. Ironically, my mother gravitated towards joy and never feared it.

My mom loved to laugh, and she had a way of filling the room with laughter. She knew how to have a good time without anything other than family, music, and good food. There wasn't a place she didn't step into where she didn't become the life of the party. The funny thing is, you couldn't even tell how unhappy she was. Beneath the laughter, there was hidden sadness. The real joy seemed to bloom when she was with her family—her parents, siblings, nieces, and nephews. She always looked most comfortable and free to be herself with them. This is where she would wind down and take off the superhero cape.

My sister and I spent time with Mom's family after school. These were the ultimate gatherings with aunts, uncles, and cousins. It was loud and wild, and all of us cousins would use this time to run rampant through the backyard. These after-school visits came with a bonus feature. Grandma's white rice and fried, crispy *mulitos*—mulitos are drumsticks in Spanish. It was the best!

Hanging out with the cousins was fun, but here is the catch—my cousins were a different breed. These kids were daredevils and scared of nothing! They were a fearless bunch. Fun for them was turning thick plastic garbage can lids into sleds and using them to slide down the unleveled, wooden front steps of Grandma's house. Meanwhile, I anxiously inspected the steps before it was my turn to slide down, hoping I would still have my life after the stair trip.

I remember this wild adventure where we wandered into an abandoned house's backyard. They found this weird berry tree and fearlessly ate the berries. They offered me some of their wild berries as if we were having a snack during story time. *Shooo*, I was still scared to eat the green part of the strawberries because I thought that part was poisonous! What made you think I would be brave enough to eat those berries that I sure as heck didn't know if they were safe to eat? I was petrified! So, I did not eat the berries, y'all! And in case you're wondering, they didn't die as I imagined they would.

We went on another expedition through another abandoned place. This time, it was a Catholic School. It seems like "abandoned" was the theme of our explorations. We ran through that school like little wild thornberries as we grabbed school supplies for our play school. They were so crazy, and their bravery knew no bounds. It never failed that when it came time to do something on their brave list, and I had finally worked up enough nerve to agree to do it, they would switch it up on me and add scarier things to the plan. Afraid to be labeled as a punk, I did everything they asked.

If you haven't noticed, I was afraid of everything. I feared that I'd fall and scrape my knee, or God forbid, that I would sweat out my meticulously blow-dried bangs that were held down by the invincible Aqua Net hairspray. Or, even worse, get them wet while running through an open fire hydrant during the summer. As I am sure you can tell, I liked safe fun. That safe fun consisted of TV shows like Wild & Crazy Kids, Rugrats, calm and organized activities like puzzles and coloring books, and things that, in my view, didn't require the courage of a lion.

Spending time with my mom's side of the family was fun, adventurous, and always so unpredictable. I'm not saying I didn't enjoy spending time with Dad's side of the family whenever we were with them. It just felt different. Unfortunately, when we did hang out with Mom's family, it had to be scheduled and approved by my dad. He had a tight grip on Mom's freedom, and he didn't like her spending time with people who might remind her of a world beyond his control. His need for control deeply affected their relationship. I am sure that it killed the love, affection, and healthiness that should have been at the foundation. If love and affection were demonstrated, it only seemed to be randomly expressed as my father's desperate attempt to mend the fractures in their relationship. Probably because at that point, when my father used these things as tools, my mother had already threatened to leave him, and the fear of losing her for good forced him to chug a bottle of "act right."

This is when my father would become a different man for about two weeks, then slip back into his old habits.

However, our life wasn't always void of joyful moments. There were sprinkles of happiness, like our family movie nights and trips to Blockbuster that included some good junk food. Christmas held its magic, too. Dad would drive us through the city as my sister and I *oooohhhh'd* and *ahhhhhhhh'd* at all the twinkling lights in the neighborhood. But over time, the bad memories began to overshadow the good ones. Each year, adding a few more memories to the pile, and soon, the bad ones were all I could see.

As I got older, anxiety, fear, depression, and anger became more familiar emotions and became permanent additions to our family. They showed up when the arguments started and would linger until these disagreements spiraled into heated shouting matches, cursing across tables, and fights in the car and even in the middle of traffic. They would make themselves known during dinner. They would pop up during our family movie night and family events. Their presence would eventually grip us all in one way or another. Many of these situations, which impacted my sister and me significantly, stemmed from an underlying issue. The underlying issue was... Control. Because of this very thing called "control," I promised myself as a young girl that I would never live my life submitted to anyone or anything that would reduce my worth and make me feel like a doormat.

Life With Mom

My mother is one of nine siblings who grew up poor with just the bare necessities. Her father was an alcoholic who verbally and physically abused her, her siblings, and her mother. To this day, I know my mom has not shared all the details of what happened in her childhood. As I imagine, it is probably painful to relive. I remember asking my mom how she remembered her mother as a child, and she described her as a "just-getting-through-the-day" kind of mom. She cared for her children because she had to, not because there was any joy in the journey. As a mom, I know the challenges of caring for children. Yes, it is rewarding, but there are moments when it can feel utterly exhausting, and that's with me having a support system.

I can't even begin to think of all the struggles my grandmother experienced as basically a young Puerto Rican single mom on the island. Just think about it? She had nine children with different needs, and no matter what challenges she faced, she had to get the job done and do it alone. It sounds like a perfect recipe for disaster if you ask me. But this was the culture, especially back in the day on the island. It's not how it is nowadays, where women have a voice and options. Back then, the option for the women was the home. Women were expected to tend to their husbands and children. They were assigned the responsibility of cooking and cleaning, and maybe if there was anything left for themselves, they could care for themselves, too. Or the mom would have to work, and the siblings would take care of each other. The weight of all that responsibility is carried upon the weary back of a tired mother. I can see where that attitude of obligation could have come from. Having a father who was deep in his addiction only made room for the abuse to get worse. Leaving them all with no choice but to do whatever it took to get out. From what I know, many of Mom's siblings left home young. Their outlet? Relationships.

Mom left home the moment she saw what looked like an opportunity. That opportunity was my dad. They crossed paths in 1988, during Stevie B.'s "Spring Love" days. Spring love was exactly their kind of love, which only lasted for a season.

Growing up, I saw Mom deal with so many challenges. Yet, I never remember my mother dumping her frustrations on my sister and me. Instead, I remember her as a gentle, tender-hearted, sensitive, and nurturing mother. She possessed many strong and beautiful characteristics like humility, long-suffering, and an enduring spirit. She was a survivor. She had, and still does have, a resilience that very few people are naturally born with. In my eyes, she was practically fireproof. Like anyone else, she had her moments, but her good days outweighed the bad ones. She always maintained an optimistic attitude. Stressing the importance of counting our blessings. I watched her turn hardships into valuable life lessons and squeeze hope out of almost everything. "Others have it much worse," she would remind us. I can still hear her saying, "Well, *Mija*-what are we going to do? At least we have a roof over our heads and aren't hungry." These words that Mom spoke held so much simple wisdom yet so much depth. It keeps me grateful when I'm on the verge of complaining and losing sight of all the blessings before me.

She always made an effort to create good memories. She did this by surprising me with mini-daughter dates after school. After school, we'd catch the bus to the hair salon. There, she'd have them give me a good trim with a bomb Dominican blowout, followed by an early dinner at a Spanish restaurant we loved called *"Ramirez Restaurant."* During school holidays and summer vacations, she would take me and my sister out to what we called in a Spanish accent *"El Secon"*—a second-hand store. This is similar to how Spanish-speaking folks say *"Walmal"* for Walmart. After the *secon* trip, we would head out to a cheap diner called *"Sam and Vera's,"* ordering full meals with drinks for about twenty bucks. Times have changed!

Whenever my birthdays fell on school days, she would send flowers to my school, and I'd receive those attention-grabbing intercom messages during class, "Can you please send Carmen to the office?" And sure enough, I would find a vibrant, colorful bouquet with a card and a balloon waiting for me. Even with limited resources, she made things happen and never made us aware of what those sacrifices cost her.

With only a 10th-grade education, my mom did what she needed to do to nurture my development as a child. Those summer nights before bedtime are still etched in my mind. After tucking me in, she read out of "The Little Golden Books" in her Spanglish accent. She was a good mom even though no one taught her how to be a good mom. If you're a parent, then you know there are no guidebooks available when it comes to being a parent. Sometimes, you learn as you go. But despite all the things she hadn't learned as a young mom and all she wasn't taught as a young woman, she excelled. She loved my sister and me the way no one had loved her as a child.

She'd wake up at the crack of dawn, taking buses to and from work, crisscrossing town on the bus route to pick up my sister and me from wherever we were. If she couldn't do it on the bus, she would rearrange the schedule because she would have to do it on foot. She was a go-getter; she was everything to me. That's why, when this image of her crumbled later in my life, it was incredibly difficult to accept that she became someone I didn't recognize. I wondered, *"Where did Mami go?"*

Life With Dad

My dad is the eldest of four siblings and comes from a hardworking, responsible, disciplined, and diligent family. His family shaped his character and instilled these values, which were passed down to my sister and me. However, when it came down to personality, my dad was the total opposite of my mom. He was rough in his speech, and his delivery was always so harsh. He wasn't openly affectionate or friendly. He was very guarded and private. He embodied what some Spanish folks call "*Machismo*." He would often say when questioned about anything, "*Porque yo soy el hombre de la casa y yo pago los biles,*" which translates to, because I'm the man of the house, and I pay the bills. My way or the highway was his life mantra. He demonstrated love and affection to us through provision and stability. The times he did show love and affection in a way that we needed it, it was always short-lived because of his short temper. It felt like he would pull the joy barometer out right when I finally felt safe enough to let loose and act like a kid.

He didn't bother to acknowledge that our feelings were hurt over something he brutally communicated, almost like he forgot how fragile we were as young girls. He just expected us to get over it because he was over it, and I had to pretend everything was okay. Despite how my childhood experiences shaped my view of my father, there is that side to him that still amazes me. He has this unique ability to perfect everything he touches, thanks to his autodidactic gene that he passed down to my sister and me. It seems to be something everyone on his side of the family carries. Along with their profession, they are also skilled musicians, writers, singers, and craftsmen. If they ever wanted to, they could start their own community with all the skills they possess, and they would be just fine all by themselves.

My dad happens to be the one in the family who is the handyman of the handymen. He was and still is a car mechanic without any schooling. His schooling comes from the books found at the auto-part store and hands-on training. Listen, there was no such thing as "YouTube University" back in the day, either. My dad can sew clothes and curtains. He can blow dry hair. He can play the saxophone, the accordion, and the guitar. He is a plumber, painter, electrician, landscaper, and a carpenter. He is skilled!

I remember seeing him putting one foot in front of the other to measure the square footage of a room while counting in Spanish. *"Uno, dos, tres. Esto es..mmm como tres pies"* One ,two, three, it's about...hmm three feet. Then, he would yell at me because something I said interrupted his concentration and threw off his measurements. These are a few things that I laugh about as an adult when it comes to my childhood with my dad. May I add that all his guesstimates were remarkably accurate, too?

He drilled division into my head during my 5th-grade meltdowns with math. It was not the most pleasant experience, but I passed math that year! My dad is a hustler and never turned down an opportunity to make some extra cash. I'm still so surprised at how much he can do. I can't even list all of his talents because there are too many to list. I'm sure that they don't make them like that anymore. And no! You cannot find these kinds on Amazon.

My dad was the one who introduced me to all the best junk food that ever existed. I'm talking Bugles, Cheese Combos with some *Malta*—a Puerto Rican non-alcoholic malt beer—Chunky Chocolate Bars, Biscotti's, Boston Baked Beans, and Cracker Jack Popcorn. YYYYEEESSSS!!!! (in my opera voice) I still dibble-dabble in these snacks from time to time. But I might have to pop some Pepcid afterward because my stomach isn't as tough as it was when I was seven!

We would eat these snacks all while watching *Silk Stockings* and *Tales from the Crypt* on TV. These are not kid-friendly shows, but I'm sharing the memories here. Although we bonded over these things, I wished we had bonded over other things like quality time. Because we didn't have this, I felt I couldn't go to him for comfort. The exception to that was only when I was sick, and that was only when I was very small. It felt like he never denied me access when I was in that kind of condition. I remember sneaking into my parent's room in the dead of night. I would find my way to his side of the bed and snuggle up with him. Those were the best nights. Just a girl and her daddy. He was a great dad when he wanted to be. Moments I still remember and hold onto.

As much as I did and still do admire all his gifts, talents, and qualities, I would have only wished that he could have been more present and emotionally available for me as a little girl. I see how my kids react upon hearing their dad's car rolling up in the driveway. They run to the door, yelling, "Daddy!" with so much excitement; you can hear it bubbling up in their voices. My husband matches their excitement by greeting them at the door with a funny, creepy voice, a tickle, a joke, and a hide-and-seek game, filling our home with their baby giggles.

Most days, when I greeted my dad at the door, he usually said, "I just got home. I'm tired; give me a minute!" The reaction to Dad getting home went from "Yay, Dad is home, and maybe he will be excited to see me today!" to "I'm not even going to bother because I don't know what to expect." As a result, I began to feel like a burden, like another thing he was trying to find relief from. After hearing this for several years, the excitement faded, and I stopped making myself available for the rejection.

I do believe that my father suffered from deep depression and anxiety. And I believe it was a generational thing, considering that I have seen the same traits within the family—including myself. Ever so often, my father would open up about his childhood experiences, which hinted that there was some trauma he might've endured. I could tell from his expressions that there was still pain, anger, and lingering bitterness he hadn't managed to let go of and deal with. I know for a fact that if my father had sought the help he needed and worked through these issues, he could've been a better man for himself and us.

I understand that many of us may have grown up in environments where seeking help for these types of things was stigmatized. We have been trained to perceive help as an intrusion and an opportunity for possible humiliation. I think that we have taught ourselves to resort to unhealthy coping mechanisms, even if they ultimately harm us and our loved ones, especially in my culture. It's no wonder that so many families end up broken and dysfunctional. We need to prioritize mental health as we do with other aspects of our lives. Your soul must be well. God wants your soul to be well.

I want to clarify that valuing the expertise and medical opinions of those in the mental health field does not diminish our faith in God's power. I'm certainly not suggesting that we should focus on counseling demons instead of casting them out. Sometimes, it's not even that deep. Sometimes, taking care of your mental health can be as simple as addressing a hormonal imbalance or changing your diet. The point I am making is that there are tools available to aid in the process of healing, like talking, therapy, etc. It is not the source; it is a resource. Seek the Lord first on this matter before you make any decision. God should always be our first point of contact when dealing with issues in our souls.

In addition to this, I believe my father suffered from soul wounds that caused so much of the behavior we saw growing up. As an adult, I can empathize with him. As a believer, my heart breaks as I understand he was a victim. The enemies traps ensnared him, and he desperately needed freedom. But as a little girl, I couldn't see the pain and weight of his depression. I only saw a man I loved, who didn't seem to love me enough to be the father I needed. With the understanding of a child, how was I supposed to comprehend that his behavior was driven by depression and anxiety rather than personal rejection towards me?

Chapter Two

The Rude Awakening

I spent the first five years of my life as an only child until my little sister came along. Our age difference made it challenging for us to find common ground, and that sometimes made me feel lonely. It didn't help that I also grew up not having many close childhood friendships or activities that helped me enjoy my childhood as I would have liked. I had friends here and there, a few sporadic moments with the cousins coming over, and after-school visits to Grandma's house. But those moments didn't happen often, and I never developed deep bonds with anyone. Many of my conversations happened with grown folks, and much of what I heard around me was grown folk conversation. I wasn't schooled on what "child talk" should have been like. My "child talk" was grown folk talk.

It wasn't until other adults corrected me for my language that I became aware of this issue. But even then, I didn't understand why I was being corrected because I thought my language was totally normal. No, I didn't have a mouth full of cuss words. But my thought process was just too grown. Again, I only imitated what I saw and heard. "You need to stay in a child's place!" They would say. Rightfully so, sis! But no one in my home objected to that kind of talk unless it offended or worked against them.

The conversations I was exposed to were mostly deep adult talks that should have been kept for after dark. Sometimes, those vulgar arguments between my parents and other family members exposed me too much. Another thing that significantly impacted me was watching Rated-R movies that contained scenes unsuitable for children and were shown without reservations. I'm not talking about a few cuss words here and there and some action. I'm talking about those movies that had quick hyper-sexualized scenes that really awakened a different type of curiosity as a six-year-old child. A "close your eyes" order was not enough to protect my six-year-old imagination from being defiled. The restriction didn't stop me from taking a peek through the blanket. My curiosity was piqued with many questions.

I was already an inquisitive child. I always needed to know why. An "I said so" would never be enough for me to stop wondering, even if I had stopped asking. When these movies came on the scene, of course, I got curious. I was even more curious as to why they aimed for those private parts that were supposed to be "private." It may have led me to believe this was what they were intended for. But my curiosity went far beyond questions and went into motion with someone else.

This someone else was someone I was very comfortable with, and they were a few years older than I was. I don't recall this enactment being done by force, and I can't even tell you how it began. What I do remember is that after a few times of this, I started feeling uncomfortable and disgusted, as it should have felt for any six-year-old girl. I knew this was all so wrong. No one had to tell me it was wrong.

At just six years old, I lacked the language to express how I felt or even describe what had occurred. More than anything, what terrified me the most was the thought of my father discovering what had happened, and if he did, I feared he would assume it was my idea and blame me. I already harbored an unhealthy fear towards my father, and that fear only escalated with this happening. This time around, my fear of him became more about what he might have done to me rather than what he would have done for me. I longed for his security as much as I longed for him to forgive me for something he was still unaware of.

As I hid this secret inside, my anxiety grew. I was just waiting for the moment my dad would burst through the door recklessly because of what he had found out. I felt like a bad girl like I was the worst, and I didn't deserve forgiveness for what I had partaken in.

Finally, when I gained the courage to speak, I didn't run to my parents first. I just told the person I didn't want to do this anymore. I thought that this would be the end of it. However, it didn't work out that way. They threw in a curveball, possibly out of their fear of getting busted, as they were also very young. To protect themselves, they used a scare tactic of manipulation that would successfully keep me quiet. "If you tell on me, I'll tell your dad it was your idea!" As I had shared, I was afraid of my father, and hearing this person say these words instantly brought on another wave of fear. I didn't have a clue on how I was going to save myself from this or how I could stop this person from getting to my dad if they had decided to go to him first with their plan.

A short time later, I decided to tell my mom. With the types of conversations that would take place around me, I knew some things, but obviously, I didn't know them in the correct order. I attempted to tell my mom by initiating a conversation with a question. Can you get pregnant with another girl? Yeah, that was my question. It was then that she realized that something was going on. How crazy is it that this was my concern at age six? What six-year-old thinks of this stuff?

Parents, as the victim and now as a parent, I urge you to be mindful of what you or someone else could be exposing your children to. Be mindful of the types of environments and atmospheres you are cultivating in the privacy of your home. Be mindful of the open conversations that are being held in front of your children. Be mindful of what you are watching and the friends you allow to come around. Deal with your behaviors that you know are plain ole toxic. Deal with it because all of those things matter! Believe me when I say they are paying attention! They are observing, and they are learning! Get your home in order!

Most importantly, rely on the Holy Spirit to lead you, guide you, and allow Him to correct you in this journey called "parenting." We don't know it all, and that is okay! Believe it or not, our roles as parents influence how our children will have a relationship with Papa God. Choosing to follow patterns because you survived them can influence their perception of Him. Remember, we represent the heart of the Father! Your home is your first ministry!

After I told my mom what happened, we had a family meeting. At the time, everything was brought to the forefront, and so were all the boundaries that would be implemented from that point on. They couldn't sleep over anymore, I couldn't go over to their house, and they couldn't come over to mine. It wasn't even a few months later that the boundaries were broken, and the restraints were lifted. And... it started again. This happened until I was about nine years old. What was supposed to be my safe place had already been infiltrated with perversion and predators that I was supposed to be protected from, right in my very home. This traumatic event in my life was the catalyst for other perversions that would later emerge.

Chapter Three

Church, Jesus, Home & Compromise

My mother had no roots or foundation in the Christian faith, aside from her upbringing in the Catholic religion, which she wasn't really practicing. On the other hand, my father had a strong background in the church. He grew up Pentecostal, to be exact. So, our introduction to church as a family came from my dad. As a child, he was very involved, doing the whole shebang—baptism, worship, Royal Rangers; you name it, he did it! I don't know what his relationship with Christ was like as a child, but his relationship with Christ as an adult seemed wishy-washy.

Before anyone made a solid commitment to serve the Lord, going to church was just what we did as a family. Whether we truly understood the

CHURCH, JESUS, HOME & COMPROMISE

difference between committing to the church rather than committing our lives to God, we stuck with it. Memories of long, *fuego*-fire, Pentecostal services with lit *coritos*- fast church songs, hot empanadas, and cold Coca-Colas still linger. The vigil nights held on those Friday nights come to mind whenever I see a jelly donut and a cheap, thick styrofoam cup with steam rising from the inside. A hot cup of coffee and a donut was the snack they all ate after prayer. If you grew up in the *Raja Tabla Church*—(an old-school church with rigorous rules)—then you know what I'm talking about.

Although my dad was the one who introduced us to church, it was my mom who fully embraced church and made the commitment. This commitment was made when a special family member came onto the scene. They had been reshaping her idea of a relationship with Jesus Christ through their life transformation.

Before their new life in Christ, they were on a very destructive path, neck-deep in addictions, involved in toxic relationships, and survived many hardships and tragedies that most don't make it through. Their transformation was nothing short of extraordinary. Whatever they had found in Christ seemed to be the real deal. If they, out of all people, could be delivered from the hellish life they had been living. If they, of all people, could be totally transformed, then Jesus had to be real.

Jesus became real for Mom around the year 1995. I sensed something different about this church experience. The transformation occurred rapidly, and the temperature of our home started feeling a bit different. The things Mom entertained changed, too. She even traded her hip-hop Salt-N-Pepa tracks for Christian artist Marino. (who, by the way, sang the scariest song of all time called "*La Gran Tribulación*"- The Great Tribulation) But the most noticeable change was her insatiable hunger for Jesus. She was falling in love with Him. She didn't just want Jesus as an additive; Jesus became her life.

Mom took us to church every chance she had, whether it was prayer service, Bible studies, home services, or any special events we were invited to or involved in. If Jesus was the center of it, she was there. She made no excuses for not being able to attend either. All the while, she worked full-time, catching the bus to and from work, ensuring homework was done, the house was decent, and dinner was cooked before church. I don't know how she managed to do all of this and could still attend church as much as she did. It's a mystery, possibly because the church was her escape; after all, it was a place where she found community. Whatever the reason, we were in there like swimwear.

As I mentioned, my father's level of commitment to Jesus was, well, not the same as Mom's. He would be sold out some days and then others; it would be as if he had never heard of the Gospel. He knew how to do church and go through the motions, but I don't believe he had encountered Jesus. Despite my father's commitment issues, Mom was still driven to love the Lord no matter what. My dad's lukewarm attitude toward the faith never stopped her from pursuing God. The only thing that she felt had put a halt to her commitment to the Lord was that my dad refused to marry her.

Over the years, I saw her stick it out with my dad through thick and thin, even when it became clear that he wasn't going to change his views on how God viewed and defined holy matrimony. I remember seeing my mom, in faith, post-date her wedding on a paper calendar we had on our kitchen wall. She even began creating her wedding decor in advance gathering fake flowers, styrofoam balls for her bouquet holders, ribbons for her *capias-* (Souvenirs in Spanish), and working on her vision. I saw hope peeking in as she built in faith, hoping that my dad would willingly marry her. She believed marriage was the only obvious solution to her sin and that tying the knot would make everything right. Although she thought she was doing whatever she needed to do to make *this* right, I don't think getting married would've changed anything. It would have only complicated them more because the root of the dysfunction was still there. There was so much more that needed fixing, and a public vow wasn't the fix.

One time, as she once again post-dated her wedding date in faith on the calendar, my father, without regard for her faith or feelings, told her in front of my sister and me, "I am not marrying you!" I honestly don't know how she was able to get past that reality, not just once but over and over again. I admire my mother's faith and know it could have happened for them. It really could have. But my dad's pride, pain, and stubbornness were boulders. From what I know, my dad had a history with marriage, and it wasn't good. He swore he wouldn't do it again. Perhaps it was a combination of his bad experiences and unresolved pain that influenced his decision. But when you're not healed from deep wounds, it leaks into everything you touch, no matter how hard you try not to let trauma drive you.

As the years went by, the little bit of peace introduced back in 1995 began to chip away. We had tension before and with Jesus, but now the tension surrounding the church had turned up. My mother's devotion to the church and God was the only thing my dad had ZERO control over. It was the only thing I saw her stand up for without backing down. Our home became a spiritual warzone, and one day, this spiritual war crossed over from a feeling to a tangible reality.

> *"Be alert and of sober mind. Your enemy, the devil, prowls around like a roaring lion looking for someone to devour."*
> *1 Peter 5:8 (NIV)*

A church just around the block would often invite guest preachers from other countries to hold tent revival services and church campaigns throughout the year. My mom heard about an evangelist who would be traveling from the Dominican Republic and immediately teamed up with my aunt to attend. Now, my mom wasn't the type to do anything unusual. She was all about caring for her family, working, and attending church. I can't even remember her having more than two close friends my whole life, and they didn't visit often.

The revival campaign was scheduled to be held on a Thursday, Friday, and Saturday night. It was a two-minute walk from where we lived. At this point, we had already attended both Thursday and Friday's service. I noticed my dad's growing frustration with each passing night. By the time Saturday came, he was giving her hell. But his tantrum didn't stop her. My mom took my sister and me as planned for the last night of the revival campaign, totally unbothered. Everyone there was in great expectation of what God was about to do. Likewise, my sister and I awaited my dad's next move.

The Sunday night service was approaching its end. As I looked to my right, I noticed that my grandfather was waiting by the church door with a message from my dad. Dad sent a warning that if she didn't leave the church, he would come and get her. That would not be pretty, and it would be embarrassing. So, to avoid a scandal, my mom packed us up and rushed home. We barely even got through the door before the argument erupted in front of my sister and me. We knew something was off, as it was most times. But this time, it was much deeper than what we could see and feel.

That night, a heavy atmosphere hung over our home as my parents continued to go back and forth, arguing. The next thing I saw was my mom praying over my dad, and he was weeping over her shoulder. That man was so bound; he definitely needed deliverance. After the prayer, some of that heaviness lifted, and there was peace, but only for a while and only for my sister and me. My dad had no idea what the enemy had planned for him that night.

As we were sleeping, the physical and supernatural worlds collided, leaving him powerless. He saw what he described as two long, black, hairy hands forcefully pulling his soul out of his body alive. He said he knew that this spirit was taking his soul straight to Hell. My mom still backs this story up, as she experienced this with him. She said she felt the evil presence in the room. Though she couldn't see what he was experiencing, she could hear him struggling to fight back with physical strength.

She described her own experience as a state of paralysis, leaving her unable to speak or move. My mother said she gained some strength and called on the name of Jesus. She then began to fight on his behalf through prayer. It was then that the spirit released him. But the spirit was still circling in the room throughout the night. My father had many of these encounters, yet none had fully driven him to surrender to the Lord.

I've come to understand that some of these kinds of spiritual experiences can be invoked through one's actions, granting the enemy authority and legal ground to establish a foothold in one's life, as it had done in my father's.

Jesus was real enough for my parents to get it together, and He was more than able to fix it! They could've been that dynamic duo. The problem was my father lacked genuine repentance. He was unwilling to let go of compromise and kill his will. He didn't want God; he wanted God's hand. He didn't want true deliverance; he just wanted relief. On the other hand, mom lacked the willpower, the backbone, and the courage to set some things in order.

Those spiritual casualties within my family resulted from choices, compromise, and, I would even say, lack of knowledge. How were we *yes-ing* and *amen-ing* a message of freedom and deliverance in church like we knew what that was all about, and yet our home struggled to grasp the surface part of that freedom and deliverance? I want to believe that my parents wanted to do their best to introduce my sister and me to the truth despite their struggles. But what we had seen set the example that compromise was an acceptable practice in the faith.

1 John 5:17 (ESV) says, *"All wrongdoing is sin, but there is sin that does not lead to death."* This wrongdoing didn't lead me to an instant spiritual death or even a physical one, but it had the potential to kill my purpose and destiny. Seeing all of this led me to believe that we were not good enough for God to intervene on our behalf or that God was merely a God with limited power. His power to do the work in my family was not limited by His choice or design— but by our choices that tied his hands.

Section 2

Chapter Four

He Made Himself Known

Music has been the language of my soul for as long as I can remember. I love and still love every genre of music. Everything from mariachi, cumbia, salsa, and hip-hop to country, soul, and R&B. You name it; I love them all. As a kid, I remember singing and dancing almost anywhere and everywhere. I would do this in the grocery store aisles while pulling out the coupons from those little red machines. I would sing and dance at family gatherings, and many times, I made the kitchen table my stage.

As you can see, no place was off-limits. But just as I felt unstoppable, my mom reminded me in Spanish that I was poppable while yelling, *"Te voy a meter"*—as I attempted to reenact a superstar stunt. My mom was the kind of mom who freaked out over anything, and I must admit—clearing my throat—I've also inherited a bit of that trait too.

To this day, I still break out in song and dance anywhere. I'll bust a move at home on Saturday morning, known as, "*Dia de Limpieza.*" This is Saturday cleaning day in a Puerto Rican household. I will still sing and dance at family picnics and the grocery store as I am celebrating a deal somewhere in the aisle. Because, let's be real, a deal is worth celebrating, right? I mean, I have abandoned the coupon dance routine, and you probably won't catch me singing and dancing on top of the kitchen table anymore unless it's a girl's night! Stappppppp! Don't be so super saved. I'm just kidding. But I'm sure you get the picture.

As I mentioned, my father's side of the family is musical. So, music was another trait that I inherited from them. I remember us having something close to a family band that consisted of my grandfather, the lyricist. My dad the guitarist, and my mom the lead singer. My dad would pull his electric guitar out of its old, torn-up leather case with his amp and start playing any tune his fingers would lead him to play. When they started jamming, that was the part where I daydreamed about being a star while I danced and created my own lyrics to match the melody.

I had passion then. I didn't know I had the talent to go along with that passion. Church gave me the platform to marry both passion and talent, and this is where worship in song was birthed. Worship became my outlet. Worship created a space where I felt light and free to be myself. I later discovered it was the portal that directly connected me to God.

These holy connections began on Thursday night prayer services at the little Pentecostal Church we attended back in the day. Back then, there was no YouTube music playlist, worship team, lights, or theatrical smoke effects. Instead, it was just the faithful congregation gathered in prayer and intercession. Don't get me wrong; I appreciate a well-executed, anointed worship set. It's just that, in those days, things were simple and unpretentious.

Going to the altar, seeking out a corner, and praying was customary. On this one Thursday night, I came in and did just that. I found a place at the altar beside one of my Sunday school teachers. As I worshipped God, there was a sudden shift. In the middle of that pursuit, it felt like I had reached the sweet spot in God's presence. It felt much different than it had felt any other time. I had never been to this place in His presence before. I began to worship like there was no one else in the room. I sang out every hymn I had ever memorized, I yelled out every kind of praise I had ever heard, and did it the best way I knew how. It wasn't for anyone except for Jesus. That night, my mission was clear: pour out my little heart and seek Jesus. And that's exactly what I did.

The service was ending, but that didn't stop me. With tears still streaming down my small face, I kept singing as if it were the last thing I would do. I wanted to keep pouring out my affection with my heart's love songs. If that meant the world would have to stand still until I offered up my praise and adoration to my God, then so be it! This deep well of worship I had discovered that night in His presence left me craving more of Him. I knew then that there was more to God than I had been experiencing.

Over the next few years, through encounters just like these, God began revealing Himself to me with clarity through dreams. And just FYI, dreams are not just your brain creating stories and your brain processing your daytime feelings. It is a very Biblical way that God speaks to man. Let me show you!

God spoke to Joseph in a dream about the birth of Jesus. (See Matthew 1:20) He warned Joseph and Mary about King Herod in a dream. (See Matthew 2:13) He spoke to Joseph, Jacob's son, about the future in dreams (See Genesis 37:9). He brought a warning to King Nebuchadnezzar in a dream (See Daniel 4:1-18). I can give a million and one examples of how God spoke to man in dreams. God is still speaking like this today and has been doing this since the beginning of time. Case in point!

I found myself experiencing more vivid dreams almost daily, with the ability to remember every detail. Sure, some of those dreams were because I had some Andy Capp Hot Fries and cookies before bed. But many of those dreams were prophetic. Some served as warnings, some came to fruition, and others felt like personal invitations from the Lord to go deeper. Our church during that time was open to much of the prophetic. This made it easier for me to acknowledge these dreams as a God thing rather than a product of my imagination. But they often struggled with knowing how to nurture and develop this gift.

It truly fascinates me how God uses dreams to grab man's attention. Let us take this a step further and ask. Why would a Great, Holy, and Sovereign God even be interested in connecting with imperfect, flawed, inconsistent men and women like us? I'm sure there are many answers out there to this question. But I answer myself with a response like this. God created human beings in His image and His likeness. (See Genesis 1:6-7) He didn't speak us into existence like the rest of the creation. He hand crafted us. (See Psalms 139:13-16) which means that we are personal to God. He created us with His heart, with His love, and a need to have a connection to Him and oneness with Him. This could explain why God would go out of his way to ensure He gets our attention even though we are so messed up. He just loves us too much to let us have our way. So, He must do whatever it takes to catch our attention because He loves us, and we are personal to Him. If you don't believe that He feels like this about you and you tend to find all the reasons why this wouldn't apply to you, then let's take a look at some of the loved, unqualified, imperfect candidates that God chose to speak to and use regardless of their flaws.

Moses was the man whom God chose to be the deliverer of the children of Israel. Moses spoke to God face to face. But he is also the one who murdered an Egyptian taskmaster. Now, let's consider King David, the warrior who cut off Goliath's head because Goliath spoke against his God. He is the same man the Lord used to relieve King Saul's torment through his anointed worship. Yet, this was also the same man who arranged for his boy to be killed to keep his wife and cover up a pregnancy. That is wild! But let me not forget to add this. My statement is not endorsing sin. All I am trying to do is paint a paradigm here. Yes, they were flawed; yes, they fell short, but God chose them anyway.

The dreams that I continued to have were like golden nuggets on a trail that kept me on this quest, needing to unravel the mysteries of God. But there was something about this one dream I had as a child that was so clear in its message—a dream I will never forget.

I dreamt that I was inside of an old colonial house. The house looked like it had been vacant for quite some time. I could tell that it was vacant and not abandoned because the condition of the house and even the furniture was still intact. Thick cobwebs clung to the wooden beams in the ceiling, and layers of dust coated almost all of the walls and furniture that could be seen. I remember wearing a long, white tunic that covered everything except my hands. But what I remember most is how the atmosphere felt.

I felt such an unexplainable peace and serenity. Nothing I had ever felt in real life could compare to this feeling I felt in the dream. I found myself gravitating towards what felt like a mystery of some sort. As I took steps to find out what this was, a spotlight would turn on, illuminating my every step. As I went up the creaky staircase, I made it to what looked like the top floor of the house. Immediately, I was drawn to a room where I noticed a light from beneath the door frame. So I thought, "Hmmm, this must be the room I'm supposed to enter." I twisted the doorknob, opened the door, and walked into a room that looked like a storage room containing memorable items. I moved toward the center of the room, stopped, and stood still. Suddenly, an overwhelming sense of peace washed over me, and a tangible presence filled the room. It was as if I could physically feel God in the room with me.

Then, I saw two enormous hands descending, and I heard a clear, audible voice—the voice of God. His words carried strength and authority, yet they were warm and gentle, making me feel safe and secure. Somehow, I just knew that He could be trusted. He spoke to me and said, *"Seek me, and the gifts will fall upon you."* I watched as gifts of all shapes and sizes, wrapped in vibrant royal colors like purple, gold, blue, and silver, fell upon me like light feathers.

Along with the gifts, there was a substance in the air that looked like glitter dust, making this dream feel more like a supernatural experience. This experience surpassed even the most joyful Christmas I had experienced as an eight-year-old little girl. I held on to this dream, understanding that God had extended an invitation to meet him first in the secret place. Then, the second part of that message was that, as a by-product of my intimacy with him, I would receive all those spiritual gifts I had desired, along with instruction and a better understanding of why I needed them.

From a young age, I have always desired to be deep with God. Not only did I desire God's presence, but I also desired the spiritual gifts that came with having a relationship with Christ. You are probably wondering, "You were eight years old kid. What kind of gifts could you have wanted anyway?" Well, I can assure you I wasn't asking for toys like the new Baby All Gone doll or the latest Polly Pocket that flashed "BUY ME!" on those TV commercials.

But as the years went by, the enemy exploited my vulnerabilities. Where the need for affirmation corrupted my pure heart of worship and unadulterated love for Jesus. I used my gift to seek self-glory because of how it made me feel and how I was viewed in the eyes of man. This self-centered pursuit eroded my intimacy with Him and brought down my time with Him to nothing. And to think this isn't even an uncommon thing among many prominent worship leaders today. People who have been serving the Lord almost their entire life at that. They lead worship, preach, and do Christian speaking engagements; they serve in all capacities without intimacy with the Lord. And people will go bananas over the skill and gifting and say," Wow, what an anointing," when it's just skill!

As it says in Romans 11:9 (KJV), the gifts of God are without repentance, meaning you can still live neck-deep in sin and still have your gift. Maybe some folks won't understand it, but I have seen it. Again, the gifts are without repentance, but that oil. Oh, that oil costs! You need the anointing to break the yoke! You can sing people off their chairs and teach theology like it ain't nobody's business, but if you have no oil, you are ministering to their emotions, not their spirits.

The broken parts of my life became a breeding ground for the influence of what I can only describe as an "Orphan Spirit." In my case, it was generational. I observed this spirit's patterns in others within the family, but it was never addressed or dealt with. So, it found a cozy place within our bloodline, making its way into our family. This spirit only magnified the already present dysfunction and tainted whatever zeal and purity I had left. The Orphan Spirit made me believe I had to compete to be noticed. If someone did something better than me, I felt the need to outdo them. I feared being replaced, which was something I couldn't bear. This made me envious of others and hyper-focused on performance and perfection.

I found myself enslaved by the pursuit of perfection, and this mindset would not allow me to embrace the belief that God saw me as His daughter without the need for constant striving. How could God love me as they claimed He did? How could He continue to see me as a daughter, unaffected by my disobedience? How could He desire a relationship with me despite my imperfections? I wrestled with these questions, influenced by a perception that was shaped by the strained relationship with my father, where I felt unloved, disliked, and unwanted due to my shortcomings. In reality, God did see me, love me, and saw me as His daughter all along. Religion had a lot to do with this flawed perception. Although I felt this way towards God, He continued to send many to demonstrate the opposite. These people served as reminders of God's affirmation, love, approval, and acceptance of me. Despite my struggles to see beyond my perceptions and assumptions about Him, God still revealed Himself, never leaving me, although I would leave Him.

Closing Out on Jesus

Our church was a small Pentecostal Church led by my father's uncle and his wife. The congregation consisted of about twenty faithful members with children. Shortly after we began attending this church, there was a pastoral transition, and a new set of pastors came in to take over. They brought their entire family on board, ready to put their hands on the plow. Over the eight years they were in our lives, they introduced the fundamentals of Christianity by emphasizing the importance of prayer, fasting, and reading of the word. They introduced Bible studies, church camps and created some of my all-time favorite church childhood memories, like trips to *"Six Flags"* and, back then, what was called *"Riverside Amusement Park."* They would also take me to what was the most lit toy store called *"KBToys."* This was way back when Baby Nanos, Tamagotchis, and Giga Pets were a thing.

When these new pastors stepped in, they bridged all the gaps. They were the head leaders for all the active ministries within the church. They helped to develop what was praise and worship at that time. Much of our song selection came exclusively from the *"Himnos de Gloria Y Triunfo"* hymn book. This is the Spanish hymn book of all the hymnbooks. They were the foodbank, the prayer team, the teachers and preachers and the babysitters. You name it, they did it! They did all of this while balancing their personal lives, too. I honor them for that because, despite their busy schedules, they showed immense love and affection toward me and my family. I always felt loved by them and they became family.

Like most of us, the pastors were not perfect. I can only imagine the weight they carried as leaders. However, I will say that while I understand that they were human, the "man's religion" that was enforced from their end played a number on me. Within this church, many things were seen through the lens of what I would call "man's religion" rather than through the heart of God.

In my view, man's religion focuses on the relationship from Man to God rather than God and Man. It exhausts people with rules that often have little to do with the new covenant that God established. It places burdens on individuals that they were never meant to bear. All this "man's religion" did was instill fear in me about committing sins, but it never corrected my mindset regarding sin. Although I had quite a few experiences with God, I had based my love for Him on how well I adhered to the rules of our religion.

These rules had nothing to do with maintaining a healthy relationship with Christ and everything to do with Bible verses that were taken out of context. Man-made religion had led me to openly embrace condemnation without realizing that this is what I had embraced. Their definition of holiness was first tied to your outer appearance versus your heart posture. This religion had a way of taking the simplest of things that that came with being a woman and called it vanity. If I cut my hair, and it was noticeable, it was a sin. If I colored my hair and wore it in a way that followed the trend of my time, then I was accused of being worldly. Even simple jewelry, like a necklace or bracelet, anything beyond a watch and wedding ring, was considered sinful. If I wore a sleeveless shirt without a shirt underneath, that was considered immoral, provocative, and sinful. I was so messed up by these religious rules that even when I wanted to do any of the ordinary things that came with being a young girl, I could never do them peacefully. I was always worried that Christ might return and find me "unprepared" due to my appearance not being "holy" enough.

I often questioned why it was so wrong for us to do these things while other fellow believers in Christ, whom we considered brothers and sisters, engaged in these very things they considered "unholy," yet their relationship with God was never discredited. Did they silently believe that they were going to Hell for not practicing the rules of our religion? To add to my confusion, one of the church leaders I trusted for spiritual guidance told me that because I had met Christ within this religion, my life would be judged by God based on its regulations. Talk about trauma! The worst part is that I wasn't the only one affected by these very things.

Many of the kids I went to school with were in the same boat, and we were teased for it, too. I didn't know all of them personally, but you could spot us from a mile away. I mean, come on, who couldn't! We were the only kids wearing jean skirts and Reeboks classics all year round! Yes, that means the winter, too! Thankfully, I was still allowed to wear jeans to school. But the others, *ay bendito*—bless their hearts! At one point, I do remember my parents attempting to apply this religious dress code entirely, and this is where my mother got super extreme. She took all my jeans, threw them in the trash, and poured bleach on them to make sure I would never wear them again. The church trauma was real! Again, the church trauma is real yall!

Pero the trauma for the *nenas!!! ¡Ay, bendito!* - For the girls, Oh lawd - The girls had it bad! Most of us had long hair: no jewelry, no ear piercings, or nail polish. The closest thing to permissible nail polish was that marble white that was barely noticeable. *Y cuidao-* And careful, as two coats of this nail polish would be too noticeable. God forbid they got caught wearing those raggedy Hanes sweatpants outside the gym. *OLVIDATE*! - Forget about it; we would be doomed. No one could understand why we had to go to such lengths. I'm not saying the church was wrong in everything it did. But if you're telling me that wearing selective items of clothing will send me to a place separated from God while you're going to heaven because of your belief in what you deem as "holy attire," I don't know about that. Something doesn't add up! If it's your conviction, that's fine. But imposing that it is the only way to be right with God, or else you're in sin? Nah, that's legalism.

Anyway, as much as we were teased and misunderstood for our dress code, we were also talked about for other reasons, and it wasn't for anything good. No "blessed are those who persecute you" existed in this scenario. We were talked about because we were seen as hypocrites. Some of us kids were only committed because we were forced to. But we had checked out long ago. We were talking and acting just like all the other kids we labeled as "heathens." Something happened that completely turned me off from this extreme religiosity, and unfortunately, my desire for a relationship with Jesus went with it. Let me tell you how it all unfolded.

When I was about twelve years old, I made a commitment to serve the Lord wholeheartedly. I was hungry for more of God and dissatisfied with the status quo. I had a burning zeal for the things of the Lord and a desire to pursue Jesus at all costs. Even if it meant conforming to this religious way of life. I reached a point where I put aside the part of me that resisted the religious rules. I stopped fighting them and just submitted. If I could have had it my way, I would have been in church seven days a week, twenty-four hours a day.

During that time, I started attending a church near my house. The very same one my father had once threatened to pull my mom out of. My mom wouldn't allow me to leave our home church permanently to join. So, I worked out a fair schedule that consisted of going to church like... every day! I would attend our church for our main services, and then on the days we didn't have service, I would attend the other church. The youth at the nearby church had the kind of fire I longed for, and it kept me coming back. I loved going there because of how alive I felt. This church wasn't just a church. They were hosting a movement, and God was in it.

This church often performed youth baptisms, and watching these baptisms made me want to do the same. This led me to have that conversation with Mom. She was excited about this new step in my journey with the Lord. I'm sure that as a parent, it brought her joy to see what God was doing in my life. So, she did what she thought was best—she called our pastor to ask about the next steps towards baptism.

My face lit up with a big, cheesy smile, hoping that he would 1) share my excitement and be proud of me as a spiritual father for wanting to take this step and 2) be ready to move forward with the baptism. I could feel the excitement bubbling up inside me as I waited for the answer while Mom was on the cordless phone that summer night. I couldn't understand why the conversation was taking so long. It shouldn't have been anything other than a yes. But as I waited for an update, my initial excitement turned into concern.

I overheard Mom's side of the conversation with our pastor: "Okay, pastor, no problem. I understand." I didn't even wait for her to hang up the phone before I asked about what he said. There was a sigh, and then she began to unload. Immediately, my stomach began to turn. I couldn't believe what I was hearing. Our pastor responded, "I don't think she's ready; I feel like she isn't showing enough spiritual fruit." What! Enough spiritual fruit?! I had suppressed every desire to do evil. I sought God the way I thought I was supposed to, and still, I wasn't doing enough? And I did it with all those *raja tabla* rules?! (Rigid religious rules) Sadly, that fire, that zeal, that hunger died. Just like that, I was done!

Yes, man's mistakes shouldn't interrupt our pursuit of Christ, but I was twelve. I didn't know any better and I don't blame my mom either. She trusted their leadership as I was trained to trust their leadership and heart behind their decisions. Still, hearing this made me feel like I was never going to be able to get it because they said I wouldn't get it. I was so turned off by this experience that it took a great deal of energy to keep me interested in wanting a relationship with Christ. This was the first time I had ever experienced what we call "church hurt."

The thing about church hurt that many tend to overlook is that it is painful. It's just as painful as a breakup. Often, when people experience church hurt, they may distance themselves from God due to the mistakes of others. Such as the discovery of character flaws within someone they had respected and admired as a spiritual leader. Sometimes for worse reasons than that. May I say that I'm addressing real church hurt? It's not the kind that people label as church hurt; and in reality, it's them avoiding accountability. The church hurt I experienced as a child made me distance myself from God, even though this was a time when I needed Him the most. I didn't acknowledge this then, but I know Jesus wasn't the one to blame; it was man's actions, and there's grace for that, too.

As for my mom, she didn't know how to help me work through this church hurt. She thought she was doing what she was supposed to do: "Honor the man of God." She probably didn't even realize that what I was going through was church hurt. Still, I silently checked out and turned to things that seemed much easier to accept and walk out, often referred to as what the church called "The world." I figured if the only way to live for Jesus was to accept all these religious shenanigans while enduring oppression from the one who is supposed to give freedom, then I didn't want any part of it!

Chapter Five

The Beginning of the End

Mom entered a season where she discovered the best version of herself. Full of ambition and confidence, she began to do things she had never done. This transformation began unraveling once she secured a job at a mortgage company. With this newfound financial stability, she bought her first car and finally obtained her driver's license. This had been one of her greatest accomplishments. However, with this new season emerging, she slowly but surely started putting her church-centered lifestyle on the back burner, too.

This caused our church attendance to drop significantly. I was already done with church, so I wasn't bothered by it. However, I'm sure the church knew something was up because of our attendance and what they saw when they ran into us in public. They would give us a sour "God bless y'all" as they eyeballed me from top to bottom. *"Carmencita se está enfriando!"*

This is Spanish church lingo for "Carmen is backsliding." But for the record, if I wasn't on fire for Jesus, it had nothing to do with what I had on people!

Eventually, I grew tired of hiding from the church, and one day, I showed up to pantomime practice with my jeans on. I was pretty sure that I would be on church discipline forever after that bold move. But this form of discipline wouldn't instill in me the kind of Godly sorrow that would have brought me into repentance as they believed it would.

Religion convinces you that grace must be earned and makes you believe that God will forsake you if you don't follow all the church rules. It also teaches that a holy life is obtained by following rules to a tee. Religion is all law and no grace. But there is no way you can live a holy life without grace. Holiness is not a matter of checking all the boxes. But religion implies otherwise. I've realized that none of these man-made rules added any value to my salvation. What's disheartening is that this is still happening to people even today and it's leading them away from God.

Unfortunately, this gradual exodus would bring nothing good for our family. Only because we felt that we had to shipwreck the faith altogether to be freed from the indoctrination of religious do's and don'ts that had nothing to do with true salvation, freedom, and relationship with God.

As Mom was going through her new self-discovery, thirteen-year-old me was preparing to graduate from 8th grade and enter high school. If you can remember this period in your life, you know there was always a big hype surrounding graduation. Everyone is excited as they await acceptance letters from different high schools. In my time, everyone is taking pictures with one-time use Fuji cameras and 110 Kodaks while writing names on T-shirts with sharpies. Then, the days leading to graduation become less structured, filled with frequent practices for the graduation ceremony, and who could forget choir practice with the most iconic graduation song? You know, the Vitamin C one, "*As we go on, we remember all the times we had together.*" I might've sung that like a worship song, but you get it! Thankfully, in my 8th-grade year, we got a new music teacher with a little more vision than the others before her. She came in with something extra besides the Vitamin C song "Friends Forever." Something like "Hero" by Mariah Carey.

The new music teacher allowed me to lead one of the songs selected for our graduation ceremony. It felt like a once-in-a-lifetime opportunity, considering that singing only happened at church. Since we left the church, I no longer had a place to share my passion except through my karaoke machine and my one-person audience, which happened to be my faithful Chihuahua, who never missed a note when I sang my heart out. So, I was happy when I got that solo.

Singing was just one of those things I would keep doing no matter what was happening in life. I could sing if I were sad. I could sing if I were happy. Singing just allowed me to release. I also felt that it had set me apart, and it did. But because I knew that it set me apart and I still struggled with insecurity, it became easy to continue to use my gift to seek compliments and validation rather than using it purely out of passion. Especially during my pre-teen years, when I felt most insecure—you know, the ugly duckling stages. Side note: These were the days I wouldn't leave my house without making sure I matched through and through. These were the days when my side swoop and baby hairs had to be laid! You know what I'm saying? I was so insecure! I remember when I was in the 7th grade and had a major crush on this 8th-grader who, in my eyes, was the most handsome kid I had ever seen. Whenever he looked at me with his captivating green eyes, time seemed to slow down. When we saw each other in between periods, it always came with hugs and small talk, and my stomach would be filled with flapping butterflies. It was no secret that we liked each other, and everyone believed we were a perfect match. We actually ended up dating all through high school and had a beautiful relationship. His family was wonderful, and his mom adored me. We were madly in love with each other, and he helped me find peace in my chaotic world. What a happy ending, right? People live for moments like these.

Yeah... So, let's take a moment to pause. This never happened! (*I'm cracking up on this one!*) I had hoped this was how the story ended for this thirteen-year-old girl experiencing her first real crush. As expected, it never went any further than a feeling. But when he quickly moved on to the next pretty new girl, and it became clear that he was no longer interested in me, I took this rejection personally. I blamed myself for the rejection and believed he rejected me because I was truly flawed and inadequate. Unfortunately, confidence and self-worth were not embedded in me, leaving me vulnerable to the sting of such rejection. Ultimately, rejection is a part of life, but how you move on from it tells more of a story about you than it does about the person who rejected you in the first place.

And that right there was my issue: I didn't know how to move on from rejection. I would dwell on it and let it define me, as I did in that

7th-grade experience. Reflecting on my life as an adult and recognizing how I had encountered similar situations on larger scales throughout my adolescent years makes me realize how unprepared I had always been. This deficiency stemmed from the absence of a foundation that was meant to be established through the affirmation and validation of my earthly father. Confidence and security in my identity were meant to start at home.

Observing how my husband affirms our daughter and witnessing its impact on her reassures me that she won't navigate rejection in the same aimless way I did. It's not to say that my daughter won't encounter these types of rejection in her life. But because preparation began at the foundation, it will be easier for her to overcome disappointments just like these and not allow them to define her. Let's all agree on this: Fathers are incredibly important! Thirteen-year-old me moved on the best way I knew how, by perceiving rejection in everything. I perceived rejection in boundaries, in moments of correction, even when it wasn't the intention.

Chapter Six

Misunderstood Rebellion

Do you remember ever playing the "Telephone" game as a kid? This game is played by whispering a message to someone, and as it travels through the group, the original message dramatically changes. I'm sure you have! As I'm sure you've have also witnessed this happen in real life. It murders people's character and destroys their reputation. Sadly, I became a victim of this game in a real-life version during middle school. The rumors weren't just hurtful; they were degrading, making me the subject of sexual gossip. I won't go into explicit details, as you can envision all this entailed. But I couldn't understand how my name got entangled in all of this.

To begin with, I was a sheltered kid. At this time of my life, my outings were limited to family gatherings, and anything outside of that was closely monitored. The closest I had come to stepping out alone was a short trip to the corner store, which took me twenty minutes, and half of that time was spent walking there. Regardless of these truths, the hurtful rumors kept spreading. How did I end up being labeled as "*that*" girl?

As soon as my alarm went off for school, my anxiety kicked in full force. My legs felt like spaghetti noodles as I entered the school building. I prayed that these kids would give the chatter a break for the day, but they were relentless.

Just when I thought I was in the clear, another wave of gossip would hit, especially in classes where escaping would be impossible. They seemed to know exactly how and when to take advantage of these moments. I desperately tried to defend myself, offering every alibi I could think of. Even with that, there was always a counter-response, like, "Well, you don't need a lot of time to do those kinds of things." I tried to prove my innocence to anyone willing to listen, but no one cared. They just wanted to believe what they wanted to believe.

By this time, I was already known for singing, giving them more fuel to spice up the gossip and ruin the one good thing I had going for myself. I just wanted to be invisible. I couldn't handle the pressure. I didn't know how to make it stop. I didn't know how to ignore it. So, I endured the criticism and judgment, letting them chatter away as it ate away at my self-esteem. I felt so angry. If anything, I was frustrated and angry with myself because I couldn't stop caring about what others had to say.

Like most rumors, I thought that all of this would pass, and eventually, they would find someone else to talk about. But it didn't happen that way. If it couldn't have gotten any worse, a family member with connections to certain circles decided to stop by my house to speak to me about this rumor. When he showed up on my doorstep, I had no idea that this was what he had come to talk to me about. I thought he had something else in mind when he asked me to step out of the house to take a quick walk with him. This felt odd because I had never experienced a moment like this with him before. If he ever had anything to say to me, he would just say it! Nonetheless, I went anyway.

Once we started walking, he wasted no time getting straight to the point. The way he approached the conversation made it clear that he had bought into the circulating rumors. His concern seemed more about the reputation I had supposedly "built" for myself rather than genuinely caring about my well-being. I immediately began defending myself, but he kept interrupting me while reiterating the consequences of this lie he seemed to believe. The fact that he doubted me, and this doubt was coming from someone I considered close family, made it even more painful. I was so embarrassed.

I was afraid to tell my parents about this, fearing they would try to handle it and make things worse. Or that they would believe it. But I really felt that I could defend myself independently and thought I should've been strong enough to do so. Why was I struggling to meet a nonexistent standard? Why did I feel obligated to carry that kind of pressure of defending myself when I was still a child?

Speaking with people became uncomfortable as I wondered if they had heard the rumors, too. And to think that this ordeal wasn't even over. It moved on to girls wanting to jump me over false accusations. I would try to avoid them, but when I couldn't... I felt my only option was to continue dealing with it internally. As I walked through the school hallways, these messengers always seemed to find me, constantly reminding me that *"they"* were looking for me.

Let's go a little deeper as to why I felt like this. I didn't live in the toughest neighborhood, but I also didn't live in a crime-free one either. It was just the hood, and such environments have no set rules. We saw kids getting jumped all the time, and it was brutal. Because of that, I thought fast and found a loophole that helped me deal with it. I began lying to my parents about being sick so I could stay home and avoid school. But, of course, I couldn't be sick forever. So, I began skipping school when I couldn't stay home. That worked until calls started being made by the school, and letters were sent to the house about my absences. My parents tried to handle my terrible teens as best as they could. But honestly, they didn't know how to handle this teenage version of me. I came with a lot that they were unprepared for.

At just thirteen years old, cigarettes had also entered the scene. How I hid it from my parents for as long as I did and still had a mouth to smoke them through beats me! But I was able to hide it for a little while until I became addicted, needing more than a few loosies to hold me over. How I had even started smoking is a crazy story in itself. I dreamt about smoking before I started. I would wake up craving it, and because so many kids in my school were doing it, it became very easy to get. Smoking made me feel cool because all the "cool kids" were doing it, and since life felt like it was falling apart, cigarettes felt like a stress reliever.

I didn't have a safe place to turn to. I even struggled to turn to God because I saw myself as wicked and deserving of all the bad things that were happening to me. My dad could only see my behavior as a teen who was just rebellious, insubordinate, inconsiderate, and "*malcriada*"- *a* bad girl. Dad couldn't understand why this was happening to him rather than trying to understand what was happening to me. His way of dealing with it involved making me the topic of discussions at family gatherings as if I were the latest hot season on Netflix. This also caused me to become more resentful and unforgiving towards him.

My father was doing everything in his power to navigate this crazy part of my life through all of his triggers and unresolved junk and all of my triggers and all of my unresolved junk. All the while, he was trying to find a way to salvage his relationship with Mom. But the truth is, despite all of his efforts, things were happening on the back end that would have rendered those efforts useless. And if that information pertaining to the backend activities had been leaked, the ship was going to sink quickly.

The Runaway Attempt

One morning, as we were getting ready for the day, Mom was in the bathroom blow-drying her bangs like she had been doing for the past thirteen years. I was also in the bathroom, slicking down my side swoop ponytail and baby hairs with my giant bucket of hair gel near the sink. I'd noticed that Mom had been rather short with me and everyone in the house in the days leading up to this morning. But, this one morning, her frustration seemed to reach a boiling point.

While we were caught up in our hair routines, she said something to me over the loud blow dryer. Judging by her eyes squinting in confusion, I could tell she didn't hear my response clearly. But it was also evident by her look that she assumed I had responded with a disrespectful comment. I don't blame her; I was known for having snobby comments. But this time, that wasn't the case. Out of nowhere, she swung the boar bristle, round brush she was using to style her bangs directly into my mouth. At first, I was shocked! I was trying to figure out what she thought I had said and why she reacted the way she did. She was convinced I was purposly being disrespectful.

My mom was typically patient with me, and her reaction that morning was completely out of her character. Confirming that this was likely just a symptom of the stress caused by the issues unfolding behind the scenes. I could tell Mom was worn out from the constant drama, and honestly, I was exhausted by it, too. It wasn't just what was happening at home that was draining for me, but also the bullying I faced at school, the internal struggles with religion, and other battles I kept to myself.

In a fit of anger, I wasn't thinking about the issues at hand; I was thinking about the plan I had been contemplating for some time—the plan to run away. But where would I go? Who would I run to? I only had a few people I could rely on, and I was still a minor with no resources. I walked out of our house that cold winter morning without second thoughts about what I was doing. I could hear Mom crying as she screamed my name from the porch, but I couldn't bring myself to look back. I felt sorry that she lost her temper, but I was not sorry enough to turn around and pretend as though nothing had happened. I huffed and puffed, tears streaming down my face, and power-walked to my destination.

The destination I chose was the closest and safest place I could think of at that time—my Godmother's house. It was about a 40-minute walk across town. It wasn't even 9 a.m. when I knocked on her door, hoping she was awake. She opened the door, and I didn't even allow her to say anything about my abrupt visit; I just walked in crying. I found myself unraveling before her without a filter. I told her what happened that morning and what had been happening behind the scenes with my parents. She felt sorry for me, just as everyone did. She knew that what I was sharing was not far-fetched. This story wasn't exaggerated by an over-dramatic little girl upset about not getting her way. Trust me, my Godmother had been around long enough to recognize the patterns with them.

After getting everything off my chest, she gave me the best advice she could give. "When you're an adult, you can decide to live your life how you choose. But until then, make the best out of it." Hands down, that was the right thing to say as an adult. The issue with that statement wasn't that she was wrong. The issue was the gap between the thirteen-year-old me and the eighteen-year-old adult me I desperately wanted to be—too much time in between!

My Godmother did the responsible thing and called my parents, although I begged her not to. I wanted nothing to do with my parents at that moment. I just needed some time to clear my mind and gather my thoughts. I just needed some space! I just needed a little bit of time away from them. But I knew that the reality was that it would not go down like that. My mom may have considered it with some restrictions. My dad? Nah! He would never allow that to happen. His way of order had to look exactly how he believed it should have looked. In his eyes, I belonged right at home, no matter what happened.

My parents finally arrived at her house. My mom walked in crying, and my dad was relieved to know that I was okay. The fear of not knowing your child's whereabouts has to be one of the scariest things for a parent to experience. Still, it was hard for me to see that nurturing and protective aspect of them through this because of how we lived our lives at home. Before this incident, nothing that I felt held any weight. But now that it seemed like I had gone overboard, it was all eyes on me. Still, in their eyes, I was victimizing them with my rebellious ways.

While I tried expressing my feelings about what I had been going through, my dad didn't see my reasons as valid or my feelings as a justifiable reason to act out. He also couldn't see how his attitude and behavior towards me exacerbated episodes of rebellion. I am not blaming him for everything that went wrong, but again, he was a very difficult man. Communicating with him was even more difficult. So even if I tried to do it his way, I was still wrong, no matter what. Mom also had something to say about this. She seemed more empathetic, and I could tell she felt guilty, blaming herself for taking me to what looked like my breaking point. But she also failed to see the aftereffects of what I was being exposed to. I don't believe that she really understood that for me to be fixed, everything had to be fixed, including them.

We had many issues as a family, but I don't think we saw them as major issues. And to think that we did the church thing. This is not to say that being a Christian eliminates all your troubles. The point I'm trying to make is that we weren't having problems that brought growth. We were stuck in cycles. We weren't living the Gospel out. This proves that being a good Sunday churchgoer brings no fruit in your life. Shallow, superficial, lukewarm Christianity can't take you to deeper levels, just as it can't get you through anything deep. Your personal relationship and intentionality with Christ make all the difference.

I can't say that anyone in our circle at the time lived out a Godly standard for how a family should function under the Lordship of Christ. Most practiced methods and strategies always contained shortcuts, mixtures, or extreme religious practices. I had not seen healthy, Godly standards within the family dynamic displayed in a way that demonstrated the heart of God. And because most of our standards were embedded in religion, it felt like we would never get there.

From thirteen years old and on, all I could dream about was finding a way to get out before turning eighteen. I thought of all the possible ways to do it, too. But all the possible options were for the future. I couldn't even legally work at this age. Even if I could work, I wasn't at the age where I could earn enough to support myself. How did people expect me to wait another five years and deal with this drama? I needed an exit now! I knew that independence would eventually come, but one thing was for sure: it wasn't arriving that day.

My poor sister witnessed all of the trauma that we all created and partook in. I guess I never considered how she dealt with these things because she never vocalized her feelings. There wasn't much that she could say or help with anyway. If anything, I think these ongoing issues scared her straight. She soon realized she would have no issues if you went with the flow and complied. That strategy worked only for a while until she, too, fell victim to the same traumatic environment that had affected me.

After my parents and I talked at my Godmother's house, we left and headed home. It seemed like things would change, and we had a plan to move forward in a healthy manner, but I remained skeptical. I had seen this pattern before. But as I had suspected, everything reverted to "our normal." The normal flow included the same old fights, that familiar tense atmosphere, and new accusations. Eventually, I accepted that I had to deal with it because there would be no way out. Emancipation wasn't an option. Living with someone else was out of the question. I would have to make lemonade out of lemons.

Fast forward a few months, and I am entering high school as a freshman. I was so traumatized by my last year in middle school that I begged my parents to get a control transfer to another high school in a different district, where I knew I wouldn't see anyone I knew from the previous year. I was determined to stay focused and felt that starting in a new place would give me a clean slate. All was going well until the storm surrounding my parents got stronger. This time, my sister and I were caught in the waves, struggling to catch our breath in the sea of our family problems, finding ourselves hanging on to whatever was left from the shipwreck.

The Beginning of My Escape

I began my first year of high school in 2003, which felt significantly different from middle school. The hallways were filled with seemingly perfect, "*novela*"-soap opera-type couples embracing each other as if they were on the red carpet. The girls looked so loved, and the boys appeared to be proud of their trophy girlfriends. While I knew it might not have been as deep and romantic as it may have looked, I wanted anything that resembled "loved." I daydreamed about being that for someone. Yet, my daydreams were often interrupted by my father's loud and clear threats echoing in my head: "*¡Si yo te cojo así, tú verás lo que te va a pasar!*" If I catch you like that, you'll see what will happen to you!" He would say this to me as a warning whenever we witnessed very young couples openly displaying affection. Despite the threats of the consequences if I engaged in any of this "forbidden activity," it didn't kill my desire. If anything, it intensified my craving for what I believed was acceptance, love, and excitement. I sought a thrill and a break from routine. That break from routine came in at the age of fourteen in the form of marijuana. Adding to the cigarettes, I had already started the year prior. While some may dismiss it as no big deal, it was a big deal because weed became a gateway to other addictions.

This habit connected me with a childhood friend on a similar path. She introduced me to something more interactive than the social media of our time. Which in those days were platforms like Myspace, Mi Gente, and AOL. If you were from this era, you know all that went into creating profiles on those platforms. You had to find someone who knew all the codes to play your favorite songs in the background and scan pictures into a computer to add to your profile. It was a lengthy process, and I couldn't access any of those things to create a page. So when my friend introduced me to this new thing known as the phone chat line, and I didn't need to take all those extra steps to be a part of the social media club of my time, I was down.

This phone chat line would allow you to have live telephone conversations with people from nearly anywhere. It was a place where you could adopt an alias and become whoever you wanted to be. I, too, reinvented my identity—where I lived, what I did, my age, and even details like the non-existent car I drove, along with the dream apartment I had hoped to have one day. No one was fact-checking my stories then, so what I said didn't matter. It was a world I created for myself that wasn't real.

I spoke with numerous people in my area and nearby cities. The interactions became so frequent that it felt like a chat line family. It was an entire community. Platforms like these have rules and warnings, yet I failed to follow those rules. I kept telling myself that it wasn't as risky as the encounters on the dark side of the internet because it was over the phone. I believed I was in control and nothing would go further than intended because I wouldn't allow it. At least, that's what I made myself believe. In reality, really dangerous things often fail to appear dangerous, causing many to underestimate the risks and throw out the rules altogether.

I remember very well the day I broke all the rules. There was no school, and my parents had to work. So, my sister and I were left home alone. Our family was very close by and would check in on us often, so there was no imminent danger.

That day, I joined the chat line earlier than usual and entered a "live room" where up to ten people could talk simultaneously. The room was maxed out and rowdy. There was someone in the live room I'd never spoken to. I thought he was new, but he was just new to me.

He introduced himself, and there was some small talk among and he invited me into a private chat room. I was obviously young but, more than anything, very naive. I didn't know much about boys. Sure, I had picked up some lingo from others that made me sound more knowledgeable, but I was still entirely oblivious and very gullible. Our conversation innocently began with small talk and laughter, completely harmless at first. Then, out of the blue, he told me he loved me. My initial reaction was, *"Bruh, have you lost your mind!"* But then, after he said it a few times, it sparked those emotions that made me feel all those things I wanted to feel. So, I just said it back. I can't even explain why; I just said it back. It was so fake from both ends. Nonetheless, he gave me his number, and we began speaking daily.

Now, remember that this chatline was used as something fun to do. It was never meant to go beyond anything other than that. But since he was a little older than me and we had been talking as much as we had been, I felt it was time to talk with him about my real age. When I told him, he was taken aback a bit, but his response was never a definite, absolute "No! We can never talk again." From this point on, we will call him Jayce. This "relationship," continued as such.

Our way of communicating was mainly over the phone and by mail. During this era, long-distance calls on landlines cost extra. It wasn't a service that came with your landline unless you paid the additional cost. And that wasn't happening in my house. So, I had to buy calling cards to make long-distance calls. Camera phones weren't very popular then, so mail was the way to go for picture mail. I had to wait nearly a year to receive a photo from him, just one picture, to see what he looked like.

Based on the types of conversations we were having, I thought we were official, you know, the real thing. Jayce was my boo. Since we were in different cities, I went a long time without putting a face to the voice—almost two years, to be exact. As ridiculous as this felt, I loved the exclusivity that he was giving me.

I was so obsessed with the idea of having love that I took it however it came, and I did whatever it took to make sure I stayed connected to him, too. I considered him a support system during this time with the issues

MISUNDERSTOOD REBELLION

that had been going on with my family. He was an escape, a safe place. The problem with this was that my parents knew nothing about it.

Ultimately, I would have to tell them because I couldn't hide it. When I finally built enough courage to tell my mom about "us," her reaction was as expected. She expressed her concerns and addressed how inappropriate this was. But her response and directive were not as strong as it should've been. Maybe she figured it was just an over-the-phone thing, and it wouldn't have gone any further.

On the contrary, when my father found out, the protective dad in him kicked in. He asked me this rhetorical question, "What can a guy that age have in common with a girl your age?" I had no real justifiable answer because the answer was, and still is, nothing! Absolutely nothing! This was one of the few times I saw my dad step up as a real protector. But boy, my stubborn, hard-headed self was committed to finding reasons why it could work. That was desperation talking. That was rejection talking. That was the search for significance talking.

My father set very strict rules on what my contact with this guy was supposed to look like—which was zero to none. My mother was also aware, and it was made very clear on what those rules were supposed to look like moving forward. However, this plan lasted only a short time before I contacted him again. Initially, it was behind my parent's backs, and then my mom became complicit.

As I reached that age where dating was appropriate, my parents considered supervised courtship. But by then, I wasn't interested in anyone other than Jayce. In my young, naive, gullible mind, I believed we had something special that I couldn't find with anyone else. Oh, little naive me. How I wish I could turn back time and change the course of my life while there was still a chance.

Chapter Seven

The Attempts

I always knew when Mom was about to leave Dad because of her language. "I am so tired of his crap." "I deserve better." "I don't want to be with him." This language I heard her using confirmed that the escape was in full motion. The very first attempt that I can remember involved my uncle. He picked us up in his 1989 purple Toyota Corolla and drove my mom, me, and my sister, (who was a baby,)around the state to find a shelter until Mom could figure out a more permanent solution.

Mom went in and out of shelters, only to come back out within ten minutes, shaking her head while she said, "They have no beds." When we left the house, it was still daylight; by the time we had found a place to stay, it was already dark outside. Thankfully, we landed a spot just in time for what they called "dinner."

The staff at the shelter led us into a huge room that served as the public cafeteria. This is where they served what I remember as an absolutey unappetizing meal. It wasn't my normal rice and beans, that's for sure! After dinner, it looked like everyone was following their nighttime routine, which meant we had to start ours, too. I could tell from my mom's body language how uncomfortable she was with us staying at this shelter. Her body language became more noticeable as we were led into this big room with many cots. I also became more uncomfortable as I noticed some of the same strangers I had seen in the cafeteria making their way into this room. It dawned on me that this room would serve as their bedroom and ours for the night. I had never been away from home, I had never been away from my dad, and I had never been around so many strangers in my life.

Before it was time to go to bed, Mom managed to get in touch with my dad. She was allowed a few minutes to speak to him over the phone. I could hear him promising to change and begging her to come back. He even promised I would get the pretty pink bike I had been wanting from that commercial that popped up on the T.V. I don't remember the result of that conversation as I fell asleep.

I was abruptly awakened by a shout and bright lights, "Everybody up!" We had to speed up our morning routine and get on the go. My mom carried my sister in her arms while she held me by the hand, and we walked through the city clueless on that cold morning. We were in an unfamiliar town where we knew no one. I wondered, "Where are we going, and what are we doing?" It felt like we just kept roaming. We passed by bodegas, bakeries, and restaurants. The windows were fogged by the steam rising from the hot food under those glowing lamps, and the aroma instantly reminded me that I hadn't eaten breakfast. I quickly asked my mom if she could buy me something to eat. She gave me a helpless look. She couldn't couldn't get me anything even if she wanted to. When she left my dad, she left with nothing. Moments later, I saw a car quickly approaching, and it looked like my dad's. Sure enough, it was my dad. He came through like the Fast and Furious, parked the car on the side of the street, and jumped out to meet us. I think about it now, and I'm grateful we went back home this time. But all that had been promised over the phone that night in that big scary room was not what ended up playing out when we got home.

My mom was with my dad for nearly fifteen years, and out of those fifteen years, I want to say she left him at least eight times. Happening the same way she had been doing it for years. Phantom-style! She would leave without a trace until she decided to let it be known where she was located. As mentioned, it always began with phone conversations, followed by garbage bags filled with all our clothes, and then there would come random trips to places we had never been to. As I got older, I was able to pick up on the signs of another great escape a lot quicker, depending on what took place prior. As more attempts followed, I didn't have to pick up on it anymore, and Mom just began to tell me flat-out.

And so, we were right here again, a few years later, where Mom was planning another escape. I was about fourteen years old when this attempt happened. It took place during the beginning of our summer break from school. My mom had scheduled to leave my dad on a Wednesday, and that Tuesday night, we went out for a nice family dinner. My father had no clue what was about to take place. Since the night went so well, he suspected nothing. The following morning, while my father was at work, she cleaned out our drawers; we hopped in a cab with our bags and met a random woman in our city with in a huge lot.

We were then transferred from the first location to the site where we would be living. We arrived at this house and made our grand entrance into what was supposed to be our new home. I couldn't see myself making this home. There was nothing homie about it. It was super outdated and smelled like an old Goodwill store.

Unbeknownst to me, this house was a home that housed women and children who were involved in serious domestic violence. They had strict policies across the board. This included how you stored your food, as we would be living with multiple families. So, we had to write our name on everything. It was so strict that we couldn't tell anyone where we were staying, and this was followed by rules applied to curfews, pickups, and drop-offs.

After they completed the intake, they led us into this bedroom with twin-sized bunk beds, a separate twin-size bed, and two dressers. I could tell by my mom's facial expressions that she was not happy. We walked in, and Mom sat on the bed, not having much to say. I could tell there was a lot on her mind. She looked so sad. If her face could speak, it would say, "What am I doing here again?" Suddenly, she burst into tears. I felt bad for her; I really did. I just wasn't sure if she would really go through with this or if she would end up going back.

Meanwhile, I was in deep thought about how life would drastically change if Mom went all the way with this. What would this separation thing look like? What would my comfort level feel like in such a controlled environment? My deep thoughts were interrupted by the phone calls that kept coming in on Mom's cell phone. Ring after ring and voicemail after voicemail, Mom was not giving in. I'm sure she had expected these calls to come in sooner or later. Sometimes, these calls were from family members checking in and making sure we were okay. But most times, it was a family member begging mom to come back for all the "right" reasons.

After only a gazillion calls, Mom finally picked up. It was the comeback call. This time, Dad had reached his breaking point, and he was about to be admitted to a mental institution. When Dad realized that Mom was gone again, he went berserk. Just picture this. My father is a petite man. But his mental breakdown must have jolted so much adrenaline in him that he became a tiny Incredible Hulk. But the *"ay bendito"* report did not faze my mom. For a second, I thought she wouldn't go back because she looked dead set on what she was going to do and unbothered by what was being said. At least, I thought she was serious this time.

That same day, we went right back home with Dad. It didn't make sense why she would go through all that trouble and panic to return. I clearly remember seeing Mom so many times, looking dead at my father's face and just telling him that she didn't love him anymore and she didn't want to be with him. So I wondered why she kept going back if she didn't love him anymore. It could've been for many reasons, like fear of the unknown. Or not having the courage to stand her ground regardless of the backlash. Even if all of her reasons were legitimate, the truth is there was damage being done because of it.

From this last escape, things started to change between my mom and me. She began to share information that, *hmmm...* maybe could've been left out. The thing is that these conversations gave me access to secrets.

And no matter how uncomfortable they were to hear, I couldn't tell anyone even if I wanted to. I knew that I had to keep them to myself. But that would also mean that if my father found out that I knew all of this information and didn't tell him about it, I would be well on my way to that blacklist no matter what I was to him. This put me in an awkward position and changed the relationship's dynamic. I don't know if she shared this information with me because she felt I could handle the truth. Or perhaps she felt like there was no one she could tell this to who would understand her and not judge her. But Mom crossed over from Mom to a friend, and I don't think I was ready for that.

As much as I was not a fan of my father, I realized many years later that these attempts also damaged him and caused him trauma. We could be having a moment of laughter, a good time with family, anything that brought on happiness, and it was not long before he would snap and say something along the lines of "For what? So, you can you leave me again?" I believe this was his way of saying, "I'm still hurt, and I don't know what to do with this pain." He was so traumatized by our Houdini moments that he silently created a checklist to predict what the day would look like. He changed things up depending on whether we were home or it was a weekday when no one was supposed to be home. If we were expected to be home, he would first run up the steps, calling out our names frantically until he found us.

Confession time! When I began skipping school, I would go back home. And because he would go home for his lunch break, I would have to hide. Nothing I am proud of, but I had to let you in on how I knew this about my dad. So, when he came home for his lunch break while no one was supposed to be there, I would hear him rushing through the house with that invisible mental checklist. I would hear him going into the rooms and opening the drawers to make sure the clothes were not gone. He was looking for clues and found relief when he knew nothing was different. So, you see, everyone suffered here. Everyone lost. Whether it was damage that had an immediate effect or something that would have long-term consequences, even if this was only supposed to impact one person, it affected us all.

My response to trauma and the way I confronted many uncomfortable situations in my life all stemmed from these events right here. They played an important role in my development, and not in a positive way. With this example of running, I, too, became a runner—whether I ran away from the problem or ran into the wrong thing to avoid facing my problems.

Section 3

Chapter Eight

The Breakup

Mom was fed up with Dad, and his tantrums weren't stopping her from doing what she wanted. She was no longer taking the high road to avoid confrontations and maintain the peace. She was evolving, growing, and discovering life outside of what she had always known. But Dad's suspicions of infidelity and his suspicion of Mom making another run for it were also growing. He often quoted this saying in Spanish that said, *"Yo no confío en nadie, ni en la misma madre que me parió*!" This means: "I don't trust anyone, not even my mother who birthed me." This reflected his general attitude towards anyone who appeared suspicious, including me. It may have seemed like a crazy accusation for my father to accuse me of knowing something more, but unfortunately, he was right.

I had the 411 on many things, and I knew what was about to take place. I knew that Mom was about ready to leave again. I was stuck between a rock and a hard place because if I had spilled the beans, it would've thrown Mom right into the lion's den. If I had kept the information to myself, I felt like I would be betraying my dad. The thing is, I knew she had made up her mind about their relationship with Dad. I also knew that regardless of Dad's efforts to improve things between them, she was going to leave no matter what!

I understood why she was decided, but I was still torn. I didn't want either of my parents to be unhappy or hurt. My dad especially. He could've been whatever he was: rough, stubborn, snobby, and impossible to love most times. But he was still my dad. In a moment of compassion toward my father, I tried to sound the alarm delicately without causing too much commotion. I thought that if I gently encouraged him to change quickly, then maybe, just maybe, Mom would've changed her mind on what she was about to do. I hadn't even finished what I was saying before he began to panic. With tears in his eyes, he immediately began to ask, "Is she leaving?" Only a true miracle would have mended this relationship, and by the looks of it, the miracle was not coming.

This time, Mom did the same thing she had done every other time. She packed all our clothes in garbage bags and disappeared. But this time, Dad didn't have to track her down and find us as usual; instead, she confronted him directly afterward. It was the first time I had ever witnessed her standing up to him like that and boldly telling him what she would do without fearing the consequences. My father didn't know what to do with this bold, confident woman who had suddenly appeared before him. This is not the woman he had known for the last fifteen years. He did what he only knew how to do. He tried to pull out every excuse, crutch, and sob story he could, attempting to gain control of the situation. After realizing that this wasn't working, and all of his words and threats held no weight and were falling to the wayside, he eventually stopped trying.

Mom moved in with an aunt as a roommate, and while this decision must have granted her newfound freedom, peace, and independence, it didn't seem to bring anything liberating for me. After she had packed up my sister and me, we were forced to stay with my dad because there was no room for us. Looking back on this, I remember being so understanding of why I had to stay with my dad. But as maturity has lent me a different perspective, my sister and I should've been included in the plan, too.

In just a matter of months, Mom was married. I was still trying to navigate the aftermath of the previous transition, and now, I had to come to terms with my mom being married to a man I barely knew. Honestly, I didn't know if I was happy or scared for her. "I told her she is moving too fast; I know, men, she needs to slow down." My aunt said. We all felt the same way. We felt like this was happening all too fast. My stepfather at the time had often recounted their love story like a modern-day Romeo and Juliet, claiming he had left everything and everyone behind just to be with Mom. This was the justification for the acceleration in their relationship.

Through my observation, his story seemed to be true. He treated Mom very well. He displayed affection towards her publicly. He consistently demonstrated his love for her without hesitation or shame. You would've thought that he worshipped the ground she walked on. I never saw my father do this in all his years with Mom. My stepdad was very kind, respectful, and considerate towards me and my sister's process of accepting him. However, as much as I wanted to turn the page on my suspicion, we still didn't have enough information to confirm if he was the real deal. I mean, he had been in our lives for...about three months? How would we have known if this was truly his character or if all of this was just a facade?

There is a saying in Spanish that goes, *"¡Tarde o temprano, la verdad siempre sale!"* This means that sooner or later, the truth always comes out...Aaand the truth came out! I knew that man had something up his sleeve, and he was too good to be true. My stepdad's story was small truths mixed with big lies. DECEPTION! He did leave everything behind to be with Mom because he saw her worthy of that kind of radical love, but it wasn't a choice he made willingly. When his last relationship ended, all of his resources came to an end as well. That's why he was there with us!

This guy turned out to be a compulsive liar. I couldn't believe the things he would lie about; it all seemed unreal. He even claimed to have a terminal brain tumor that would have left him with only six months to live! This man even went to the extent of lying about being a D.J. and a barber in Puerto Rico. And because I trusted and believed him, I LET HIM CUT MY 3A TYPE CURLS WITH SOME DULL POULTRY SCISSORS! Poultry scissors, y'all! It was an even cut, but still! Why, bro? Why would you lie about something like that?

I wasn't sure what Mom would do with all of this evidence, but as I suspected, she overlooked it and gave him the benefit of the doubt. Given all she had been through with my father, I would've thought that she wouldn't have tolerated what this man was doing. Years have passed, and I have had much time to think about this scenario and why things could've played out as they did. Why did she let this slide? Although we saw the facts as they were, I believe Mom saw it much differently. I think she believed that he loved her the best way he knew how, and because she had never experienced that level of love and affection from anyone before, she ignored the red flags.

These unfortunate events unfolded at the most inconvenient time. My stepdad was the key to the plan that was supposed to help Mom get on her feet, and that would allow me to live with her permanently. Since all the promises of getting an apartment ASAP were lies, all my future plans were blown into smithereens along with his cover. My hopes of Mom establishing her life quickly as planned were not coming anytime soon. So, living with my dad would have to stretch out for a bit longer. Mom tried to keep me hopeful with some of those positive pep talks she always gave when faced with hopeless situations. However, it didn't bring me peace like it had every other time. I had accepted that "soon" was just a placeholder for "I don't know when."

Chapter Nine

The Aftermath

Staying with Dad provided a sense of stability for which I was grateful. But I dreaded returning to that house every time. Any sense of warmth and harmony that had ever existed in our family home was quickly replaced by the heavy weight of my father's grief. His grief manifested through outbursts of anger, blame, and constant strife between us. He appeared angrier than I had ever seen him before, projecting his frustration onto me due to what I knew about Mom and what he believed I chose to withhold from him. This mainly happened when memories of my mother triggered him and led him to relive the tragedy.

When we initially left that house, I never thought I'd return under these circumstances. In my father's eyes, I left as a traitor and returned as an enemy in his camp. I knew that my dad harbored resentment toward me because of the information I withheld from him. If only he could have understood that I had no control over my mom's decisions. I didn't willingly become his Judas. But it didn't matter what I had to say or how good I was to him; I could do nothing to make him forgive or forget. He became indifferent towards me, and I could tell that, at times, he couldn't help it. Unfortunately, I had to sit there and take it because I had nowhere to go.

A time did come when he transitioned from the stage of anger into the stage of acceptance. His acceptance brought about a midlife crisis. It was like one morning, he had rolled out of bed and decided to become a new, self-improved, single, and ready-to-mingle version of himself. He started by renovating the house, then took it a step further and underwent a complete makeover from his attire to his swag. He went from tight Levi jeans and Champion sweatshirts to matching jogging suits, Cuban link chains, and bracelets. And for the record, the Champion name brand was way cheaper back then! He began his dating frenzy, and he was kicking it to whoever. He tried kicking it to the neighbor, the neighbor's friend, and whoever seemed to catch his eye. This behavior was very uncomfortable for my sister and me to watch. Seeing him in this state felt unnatural since we had only seen one side of him until now.

I would come home to find all the girls Dad had been talking to giggling, drinking, and having round table discussions in the very same kitchen my mom used to serve us dinner in as a family. And to think that these girls had nothing in common with my dad. They went clubbing, they drank, they smoked. They did everything I never saw my father do and everything he had always opposed. At that point, I would have gladly taken back the dad who just came home every night and nagged rather than this thirty-five-year-old gigolo who was going through a mid-life crisis.

During that period, there had been a revolving door of women entering and exiting our home and my dad's life. But this one woman, in particular, came under a different set of circumstances, and my sister and I could not deny that she was different from the rest.

My father planned a trip for this woman to come down and meet us. The week before her arrival, it was like my dad's behavior had become something like a dictating king, demanding perfection from his obedient servants for his newfound queen. It didn't take much for her to notice how Dad placed her on a pedestal as we watched.

He offered to pay for her nails, hair, clothes, car rentals, and splurged money on just about everything for her. What made matters worse was how he lectured us on the side for asking him to do the same for us. "Just because I'm buying her stuff doesn't mean I have to get you anything," he told my sister and me. The way he spoiled that woman that he didn't know from a can of paint is not anything he had ever done for me, my sister, or even my mom.

But homegirl was not blind to the situation. He might have thought she was just like the others, but she set him straight, specifically after learning what had been said to us in private. She told him she would not allow him to spoil her if he couldn't do the same for his girls. He complied with her demand out of the pressure of gaining her approval. That one day, Dad had no choice but to do all the girly things we wanted to do, and this had been the most we had ever been spoiled by our dad.

We got our hair and nails done; we went shopping and even enjoyed a meal without him freaking out about the cost. Even with everything we requested, it didn't even compare to a fraction of what he had invested in the various women who had entered his life during this time. I am not saying that he didn't give us our needs because he did. But nothing like this. I couldn't make sense of the clear contrast between how my dad treated us, as his own daughters, and the way he treated this woman who, at the time, felt like an outsider.

I liked to say that my father believed that love could be bought. What I saw him do for many women removed all the excuses he might have had for not treating us nearly as well, even though he claimed he didn't know how to be anything other than who he was. My father's pattern of investing in women with money and actions became a recurring theme after my mother left. This consistently made my sister and I feel undervalued. It's almost like we had to compete to get a part of him that should've already been ours. I often rationalized his lack of affection towards us by reassuring myself that he must have had valid reasons for his behavior. Mainly so he wouldn't feel guilty and I wouldn't feel rejected by him.

My Aftermath

As if things weren't already overwhelming and stressful, Mom dropped another bombshell that brought on another delay. She was pregnant and moving to another state, making herself physically inaccessible. I was extremely frustrated with her. She left me with my dad, fully aware of how difficult he was, to pursue her happily ever after. Meanwhile, I was forced to return and live with the monster she had created.

With all the stress that came with these wild transitions, I began spiraling into a deep depression, and no one even noticed. To everyone else, I was just a rebellious teenager. But on the inside, I was slowly fading, barely existing and often wondered what it would be like to not be in the world anymore. All I did was smoke cigarettes as my appetite decreased. The stress took a toll on my petite body as I began to thin out rather quickly. I was so tiny that my pants size was a size ten in little girls, and that was with sweatpants underneath to fill in. You could literally see my collarbone without me taking a deep breath.

It was hard to find an outlet in all of this, as my every move was now controlled and monitored. I couldn't go out; I couldn't really talk with anyone other than the people my dad brought around. If I took longer than he'd estimated on a trip to the store, it immediately escalated into a fight or, as we would say in Spanish, "*Un mal rato,*" meaning a really bad time. I quickly fell into the role of a mother for my sister, and I became the housekeeper. This may sound like I am exaggerating, but it's true.

I only trusted one person, and that was Jayce. He was the only one I considered a safe place where I could vent. I knew that whatever I shared with him in confidence would never reach my dad's ears. But sometimes Jayce would go through these sudden shifts in his attitude towards me without any explanation, intensifying the feelings of abandonment and rejection I was already wrestling with. This often made me feel disposable. But I desperately clung tight to him because I needed one thing in my life that resembled stability. I needed something to hold onto, something that gave me hope, and he was that for me. So, even if our relationship came with this, I still wanted it.

Through all this, my father's continuous search for "the one" looked like it had ended. He met this young woman who was in the process of getting her life in order. My father was convinced they could accomplish their goals together, and within several weeks of knowing each other, she moved in. She appeared to be the perfect wife. She cooked, did laundry, and cleaned like a military soldier. The house was immaculate for the first several weeks of her living there. You couldn't find a dust bunny even if you tried. With her coming into the picture, I felt hopeful about her being the missing piece we needed—a young, relatable stepmom who could understand us. I secretly had hoped she could be that someone I would've been able to find a friend in. But because of the many issues between my father and me, she had a tainted narrative concerning me way before I had an opportunity to show her who I really was.

I began confiding in her, sharing deep secrets like we had known each other forever. My mother repeatedly warned me, "She is not your friend; stop telling her your personal things!" But I never listened to Mom's advice. My dad's girlfriend made me believe she was a safe place. That is, until one day, everything blew up in my face. I only realized this because when my father confronted me about things, he brought up information I had only shared with her. This cast me as the evil stepchild and portrayed her as the angelic figure. Just as my mom overlooked everything with my stepfather, my father overlooked everything with her. This shifted everything. She tolerated me because I was his daughter, and his indifference towards me intensified. In turn, I grew bitter towards them—more towards my father. Watching him live out what he considered to be his best life made me angry. It didn't feel fair. He had found his happy ending, and what about me? What about what I deserved? After a while, Mom finally got a place, and that day couldn't have arrived soon enough.

Aftermath with Mom

Mom was already eight months pregnant with my brother when we moved into this one-bedroom apartment building. We converted it into a tiny two-bedroom apartment, making my bedroom the second bedroom, which was about the size of a closet. The only thing I could fit in the room was my bed, which was wall-to-wall with a small nightstand. I had a small, clear jail TV that my stepfather ingeniously hung from the ceiling using a MacGyver invention he created from a metal fan stand.

Our apartment was on the 3rd floor, and it was always so hot. The heat amplified that weird stench in the hallways. There was also an infestation of unwanted, disgusting little pests. ROACHES!!! It's not like I had never seen roaches before, but bro, these roaches came in all shapes, sizes, and colors that I had never seen. It was like this building was the designated headquarters for recruitment. My skin still crawls when I think of this! Not to mention that the building was not in the best condition. Every time it rained, the ceiling in my bedroom leaked, causing a small part of the ceiling to collapse.

By the looks of it, the city we moved into seemed much worse than where I came from. Our home ended up being dead smack in the middle of a drug-infested neighborhood. On my way to school, I would find some of the addicts passed out in our hallways with puddles of urine that belonged to God knows who.

This move brought on a new way of life that I was not used too. This wasn't exactly the new beginning I expected. We barely had anything and when we ran out, we ran out.

When we ran out we would have to wait until the start of the following month when we received our state benefits or *"cogerlo fiado"*— put it on the tab, and we'll pay it later, as Mom would say in Spanish. We didn't have many things I once considered an absolute necessity. At first, we didn't have a washer or dryer, and we definitely couldn't afford to go to a laundromat. So, washing clothes by hand with a bar of soap was the way to go.

Let me just say this: washing clothes by hand is not for the weak. Not having a washer or dryer during the winter, *uffff*, that was tough. Thankfully, my mom was from the *campo*- the countryside, and she knew how to make it through tough times.

Sometimes, I had the luxury of using my iron dryer, also known as the radiator. But sometimes it didn't dry my clothes completely. So, I resorted to my all-time desperate option, *"El blow-dryer."* But that came with its own set of issues because if too many people were using their appliances at the same time, it would trip the breaker in the building, and all of the electricity would go out. Summertime relieved some of these issues by making the clothesline open for use. I wasn't new to the clothesline, but I was new to the experience of having my clothes stolen off of it.

Among other things, I didn't realize that cable wasn't necessary until I moved in with my mom. Cable, for us, was those little corny channels that were picked up without a cable connection.

But we didn't care. We were just excited to see something on a screen. We even created a little family routine around the two programs that were available to watch. Monday through Friday at 7 PM, we faithfully rushed to watch "*Wheel of Fortune*" and "*Jeopardy*," as if they were new shows everyone was raving about. And to think, these were the rinky-dinky shows I would never allow myself to be entertained by.

But after everything I had been through in the last year, I could've cared less about what I didn't have. I had a place where I had peace, and that was enough for me. Besides having a peaceful place to rest, the added benefit was that Jayce now lived closer.

Rocky Road

From the outset, we were all headed in the right direction. My stepfather had a stable job with a consistent paycheck that could support us. I was on my grind and focused on completing high school, and it felt like Mom and I were finally redeeming the lost time. Somebody say, "All good things."

Then, the moment we had all been waiting for arrived. My baby brother came into the world, leaving my brother and me sixteen years apart. For the first week, it was exciting to experience the newness of a baby in the house.

I especially loved it. I wanted to feed, burp, bathe, and comb the little bit of hair he did have like he was my baby doll. But things took a sharp turn as a new baby not only placed a demand on us all but exposed some things that Mom and I didn't see coming. Clearly, my stepfather wasn't as responsible or reliable as he claimed.

I came to this conclusion after he came home early one day from work without a job. Still, to this day, we have yet to learn the real story behind the why, and this was not the first time that this had happened.

This latest disappointment only reinforced Mom's emotional barriers even higher than before. Adding to the stress, Mom found out she was pregnant again. The peace I had endured so much to gain had been hijacked by circumstances I had zero control over. Sadly, we never fully bounced back from this setback. There were small spaces in between where we were able to catch our breath, but it wasn't long before we were, once again, scraping for nickels and dimes.

This situation really pushed me to buckle down in school, knowing that finishing school on time was my ticket out. I promised myself that I would stick to my goals and avoid distractions at all costs. I set two straightforward rules.

Rule number 1: Don't make ANY friends.
Rule number 2: Don't speak to ANYONE at all.

I viewed isolation as a form of protection. The less anyone knew about me, and the less I knew about anyone, the better. This would protect me from ever going through what I went through in my past school experiences.

As a freshman for the second time, I was a new face, and I was what they would call "Fresh meat." Being a newbie in school, people wanted to know who I was and where I came from. This curiosity came with compliments, too. My response to every compliment I received was a harsh "I got a man!" I had only wished that this man was as real as I made him out to be.

Jayce and I were already in the second year of our very unconventional relationship, yet we still had not seen each other face to face.

It was embarrassing and exhausting to explain to someone that I had a boyfriend I had never seen despite us being so close in distance. I had befriended a few women I met off the phone chatline that also existed where I was living, and these women were older and considerably more experienced in life. Their thoughts and advice were the same across the board. They would say,

"Girl, please! If he hasn't come to see you by now, he isn't coming!"

"He is probably hiding something!"

"He is a grown man, and he is out there doing his thing."

"Mama, he is a man, and he has needs."
"You're a smart girl, and you're beautiful! You can have a normal courtship with someone within your area and within your age range! Why do you keep pursuing this?"
I had nothing to say in his defense.

Not long after I moved in with Mom, Jayce dropped some unexpected news. He was moving, too! And not to a different city within the state or even one state over. The move was several hours away. Given the obvious reasons, I was already struggling with insecurity about our relationship. Being a young girl filled with insecurities, I couldn't shake the worry that there might be a chance he would meet someone else—someone who didn't have all of my limitations. Someone who could offer him something more than I could. I didn't want to show him that insecure part of me. So, I continued supporting and encouraging his decision, believing it was what I was supposed to do. Besides, the reason he gave me for his change in demographics seemed legitimate. He was moving to establish a better future for himself. What would I have looked like, raining on his parade? But here was another concern of mine. If he wasn't willing to travel now that we were closer, was he really about to travel then? This forced me to give him an ultimatum with a deadline. In turn, he also gave me an ultimatum—I had to finish school on time.

A few months had passed since his move and he seemed to be doing really well. I was genuinely happy for him, but the lingering question remained. When was this brother coming? Labor Day was the next three-day holiday weekend approaching, and there was some conversation surrounding a trip to his hometown to visit his family. I quickly took advantage of that conversation and asked if he was coming to see me. I could tell he was getting annoyed with the same question, but I needed an answer.

Now, remember, I had never seen him in person. All I had was one photo to go by. He didn't look terrible in the picture. But let's be real: people look good, depending on the angle! So, I was hoping for the best and preparing for the worst. He could have looked better than the photo, or this visit could have been a straight catfish. I kept thinking, "If this guy turns out to be hideous, I don't know what I'm going to do!" I know, I know. This sounds a bit judgy for some. "It's the heart that counts!" they say. Listen, physical appearance does matter for some. I am not saying that this is all that matters, but no one is going to hell if they don't want to date someone they aren't attracted to! I was not Jacob from the Bible who had to marry ugly Leah, okay!

It was the Saturday of that Labor Day weekend. As I sat on the porch, I heard a knock on the door and thought, "Oh my Gosh, this is it!" In those twenty seconds from the porch to the door, I had a whirlwind of emotions and felt like my heart was about to come out of my chest. I quickly took a deep breath and opened the door. And there he was, standing right in front of me! This was the moment I had been waiting for.

It was undeniably awkward; I was unsure of how to feel or what to say. I couldn't believe that the man I had been talking to daily for the past two years was finally before my eyes in the flesh. I had fallen in love with him and gave myself to him emotionally, but after this visit, our bond solidified, and I gave myself to him completely. From then on, every decision would be centered around "our" future. Again, this is my sixteen-year-old perspective expressing my feelings and recounting the story. Grown and healthy me says, "This should've never happened!"

Chapter Ten

Down to the Wire

Music found me again, and with that, I met a group of like-minded creative folks within the area with whom I developed a friendship. With this relationship came the added benefit of free studio time. I took full advantage of what I saw as an opportunity, dedicating most, if not all, of my spare time writing songs to tracks no one wanted.

I had the opportunity to work closely with a talented local producer, and instantly, we clicked. He possessed a unique talent called "vision." He could see potential long before you recognized it within yourself. He had a way of drawing greatness out of me, always leaving me feeling encouraged and motivated about my future. He consistently reminded me of my worth, value, and the importance of not compromising on what I deserved. He was among the few who saw beyond my rebellion and irrational actions. He felt like the older brother I never had. His advice and the deep, sobering conversations we had about my future would linger in my mind for days on end, causing me to reconsider what I deemed important.

His conversations often made me pause and wonder if I was giving myself enough space and time to figure out who I really was outside of this relationship. Was I planning to run off with Jayce and let his dreams become mine? Was I even ready for that? What would happen if I ended up outgrowing this relationship? Should I have saved us the trouble and ended it before it went any further? Would I be okay if I did? Would he be alright?

I was scared of being honest with myself. I was afraid to hear the real answers to questions that mattered, fearing that it would force me to alter my plans. Sure, people on the outside might've said I was too young to be stressed about major life decisions. But despite my age, I wasn't your typical teenager dealing with everyday, regular problems. I had to figure this out now!

While the relationship was a strong motivator to jumpstart my commitment to my academic goals. It just wasn't enough to keep me disciplined to stay on track. By the time I realized how off-track I was, it was too late to dig my heels in the ground and make changes, as Mom had already received another eviction notice. Although I knew she would figure out something like she always did, I just couldn't take the chances. I couldn't afford any more setbacks, whether they were my fault or not.

After much thought, I reached out to my dad, as my last resort, asking if I could move in with him so that I could finish school. It was a bitter pill to swallow, as I had sworn I'd never return to that house, but sometimes you have to do what's necessary.

My Dad agreed to let me return with very strict rules but allowed me to move in. As soon as I moved back, I hit the ground running. I went to school during the week, did my community service after school, and was focused. With Community service, summer school, and the advantage of how the credit system operated in my hometown, I would've been able to graduate as scheduled, if not sooner.

My dad and I mostly maintained a civil relationship, and things were running smoothly. Until tensions flared up as expected. Our strained relationship caused us to lose touch with our roles as father and daughter. And this is what turned a convenient option into a disastrous one. If it wasn't our past that played a role in this, it was his constant nitpicking and complaints about anything and everything I did. He didn't hold back with his words, and that wore down my patience and endurance.

I finally reached my breaking point, and with all the issues at hand, it was evident that graduating on time would be impossible. So, rather than waiting for the unexpected, I proactively moved onto plan B. Now that I was seventeen, other options were available to finish school. And with Mom getting another apartment, this became part of my plan B.

I signed myself out of high school, moved back in with Mom, and devised a plan to obtain my G.E.D. instead. I did not have a set amount of time on how long I would be staying with her. I just knew it wouldn't be permanent.

She ended up renting a bigger apartment. But I couldn't help but wonder how she could afford it with her income and history. I tried having those hard, uncomfortable conversations that I had hoped would help her see the patterns she kept falling into. Still, it felt like I was beating a dead horse. Seeing her in this state, knowing that she could've done better, broke my heart. Somehow, she just got stuck.

Sadly, I lacked compassion towards her and felt incapable of granting her the patience she needed from me. I just felt like life had been tough on me too, and I had to learn from those tough experiences and roll with the punches. I expected her to do the same. Instead, she chose to wait things out, hoping they would get better on their own. Her hesitation to move forward might have been driven by different reasons, like the fear of repeating past mistakes. Regardless of what it was, her loss of motivation frustrated me just as much as I had once frustrated myself with this similar behavior.

I constantly worried about what would happen to her once I left. I felt responsible for her and felt like she needed me more than I needed her. I struggled with this survivor's guilt, knowing I had a way out and my mom and siblings didn't. I feared the kind of struggles that my siblings would have to confront if things didn't change quickly. I wanted Mom to have a stable home she could live in for more than just a few months. I wanted Mom to break free from the cycles she was living in. Most of all, I wanted her to believe in herself as much as I believed in her. The only thing I could do to guard my heart from this disappointment was to turn a blind eye. Turning a blind eye looked a lot like leaving.

My original plan was to stay with Mom, focus on completing my G.E.D., find a job, and save money. That way, when I moved in with Jayce, most of the surface matters would be sorted out. After a conversation with Jayce and some research, I found a school in the same area where he lived where I would execute the same plan I had set to do while living with Mom.

Let me just say this. It was never a part of my plan to move in with Jayce without having the basic tools to contribute and be somewhat independent. However, because of the circumstances, the timeline for the plan was expedited.

Before I moved, something quite interesting happened. It was an experience that my mom and I shared, one that contradicted everything about our belief in God and the practice of witchcraft. We agreed to have a tarot card reading with a witch. You read that right: a tarot card reading with a witch. It's wild how we drifted so far from our beliefs that we willingly dabbled into something like this without any conviction.

I recall the witch performing her ritual, setting the ambiance for spirits to communicate with us. As she came to a close with her preparations, a strong breeze blew into the kitchen. The witch acknowledged the strong breeze as a sign that the spirits had arrived. With their presence acknowledged, she began the card reading.

During the reading, these three cards revealed everything I had planned on doing. Strangely, I felt excited about this confirmation I had received from an evil source. But I had an unsettling feeling that something wasn't right with this upcoming move.

It's important to understand that just because someone can tell you accurate information about your life doesn't make it a good or Godly thing. Familiar spirits can also communicate through such means. So, it's important to have discernment and always check the source. People often try to mask this as a good thing because it brings clarity and appears helpful. Or they might try to downplay the fact that it isn't satanic just because it doesn't come with the stereotypical devil with two horns and a pitchfork. Listen! If it doesn't come from the Holy Spirit, it will lead you away from God. And since I was easily manipulated and had no fear of the Lord, I fell into deception.

I never shared this doubt about this move with anyone other than one other person. It was a woman I had met at an old job who was a Christian. I began letting her in on my fears and concerns. As expected, she offered me Godly advice that opposed the move. Though I was hesitant to accept what she said about my unsettling feelings, she prayed over me anyway. Against what she said, I packed my small bags and prepared to leave. I said my goodbyes to Mom and my siblings.

I share this experience, although it may seem non-linear, because I want you to understand how misguided I was in my decisions. Growing up quickly out of necessity, with few stable figures in my life, led me to seek security in anything I could find, including witchcraft. This not only opened the door to the influence of the demonic but also exposed me to many other unforeseen circumstances that I was completely unaware of until they actually occurred.

Section 4

Chapter Eleven

Our Journey

On June 7, 2006, I reached my destination. Jayce had arranged for me to get picked up and dropped off at the apartment. Although I was excited to finally be there, I couldn't shake my nervousness—not only because I barely knew the people who were picking me up, but also due to self-conscious thoughts I had about my appearance. I found myself worrying about every little imperfection I noticed and every imperfection they might have noticed, like the huge oil stain on my left Timberland boot. I couldn't help but wonder what kind of impression I was making, looking as poor as I did. I mean, I looked like I needed a sponsor. Maybe I didn't look that bad, but it was bad compared to what they looked like.

I rolled out of that train with a tiny, green suitcase that contained all the clothes I owned. The suitcase I had was so jacked up it wouldn't close, and I couldn't afford to buy one. So, Mom had invented something to hold it shut. She made a hole behind the zipper and the front flap that was big enough to loop in a scrunchie to seal it shut. I had hoped that those little pests I left behind didn't find their way into my bag, making a grand appearance on my behalf, because that would've been a *"tremendo bochorno."* Huge embarrasment! Thankfully , they gave me that "ay bendito" smile and carried my jacked up suitcase to the car.

My new home was roughly an hour from the train station where they had picked me up. I knew that once that car stopped, I would be in my new home. I assumed I would instantly feel a sense of belonging and wholeness as soon as I arrived. But upon arriving at the apartment and reflecting on what had transpired, I didn't experience the euphoria I had anticipated. The feeling of belonging and wholeness I expected to gain from this move was absent. What was present was the weight of the decision I had made, and it was starting to sink in. This was my new home, and I was now six hours away from my mom, siblings, and everything I had ever known. I suppose the transition, relationship dynamics, and my age influenced these feelings.

I had just turned seventeen years old two months prior. I didn't know a lick about being independent, let alone navigating a relationship. Jayce and I had sustained our relationship over the phone, and that had not fully prepared me for what sharing my life with him would look and feel like. For a moment, this sobering thought made me feel like I was moving in with a stranger. Nevertheless, I was already there; besides, this is what I wanted, right?

Jayce would be arriving later that night from work, and my stomach was doing somersaults as I mentally prepared to meet him for the third time since we had met in person. That eight-hour wait time flew by fast as I noticed his car coming up the driveway. I heard him coming up the stairs, keys jingling from outside the door, and Jayce then walked in with an awkward hello. I had imagined a grand, romantic reunion with fireworks, but instead, it was like a confetti popper that didn't pop and had lost its sparkle. I didn't know how to transition from the person he knew over the phone to the real-life Carmen, and it seemed he felt the same. Even our conversation was awkward that night, perhaps because we both realized that this hello would be different from the last ones we had given each other. This time, the hello was a greeting to partnership, a hello to life together, and there would be no "*ta-ta* for now" after this meeting.

Walking into this new chapter of my life meant I had to adapt to an environment different from what I had always known. Picture this: I had spent my entire life in a city-like neighborhood, and now I found myself in a quiet, rural town, a world away from the hustle and bustle I was used to. The mornings in this peaceful countryside were refreshing and a bit alarming. It was quiet enough to freak me out as a loud Puerto Rican who wasn't used to silence being something normal and safe. I was accustomed to living in a noisy neighborhood, where I would hear more than just birds chirping. I was used to hearing *Panchita* from next door yelling at her kids and the loud reggaeton blasting from someone's Honda Civic. In this town, there were no signs of the hood anywhere—no corner stores, bodegas, icey carts, or porches filled with loud people and music. And I cannot forget to mention how that not-so-pleasant country smell of manure assured me that I was nowhere near what I used to call home.

But this change had its perks, like the fact that I moved there during the summer. The timing gave me a wonderful introduction to country living.

It was a breath of fresh air, literally. The summer nights brought a calm, cool country breeze that created memories I'll never forget.

Although it was nothing that I was used to, I didn't wake up to the sight of addicts and drunks in the hallways. My roof didn't leak, and I didn't have to worry about the lights going out every time I used the blow dryer and the microwave at the same time. Everything in my apartment was intact, and there were no uninvited pests like the ones from the building where I lived. Now, that was a luxury I could've gotten used to.

The first few weeks of living with Jayce were all about settling in. He was there every step of the way, helping me adjust. I couldn't have been more grateful for his support during this transition. But it's important to remember that Jayce wasn't a friend or a roommate lending a hand; he was now my man, and I was his girl/wifey. As much as he felt the need to do this for me because he "loved" me, there was also an expectation on my end because I said I loved him too.

That's what people do for each other in relationships, right? They take care of each other. Something I had zero experience in when it came to love relationships. Now, because of my commitment to him, there was silently an expectation of me as "*La mujer de la casa-*" The woman of the home. I knew the basics of maintaining a home, but only because those were my chores, not because I took pride in accomplishing these tasks. Besides, I wasn't *Carmen del Campo-* Carmen from the countryside, who had been doing this her whole life.

Nonetheless, my inexperience didn't exclude me from meeting the cultural mandate prevalent in many Hispanic communities—it's considered an obligation, a sort of unwritten rule to comply with. The rule is simple: take care of your man, sis! Plus, if you're living together, he's no longer just your boyfriend; he's your *"marido"* – your man. Whether there's a ring on your finger or not. You must measure up to their expectations. And cross your fingers, hoping that the family never has to give you a pep talk about handling your business because that would be utterly humiliating, and the family will never let you forget about it, either.

What I grew up seeing is that as women, it is expected that you clean, cook, contribute, and care for your partner's needs; otherwise, you'd be what the women would call you in Spanish, *"a cochina, una vaga,"* and a *"tu nunca hace nada!"* A slob, a lazy woman, and you never do anything, along with many other things I can't even repeat. It was as if you were just supposed to magically know how to do everything you had no experience with. If, by any chance, someone visited the house on a messy day, forget about it; it will always be the woman's fault, no matter the circumstances.

Granted, Jayce never made me feel like I had to be his slave or wait on him hand and foot, but it is something that was expected for me to know how to do. Fast forwarding to my life now as a wife and mother, it brings me great pleasure when I serve my husband and family in this manner. But let's talk about seventeen-year-old me. Hmm, yeah, not so much! I cared about Jayce, but not to the extent that I would've felt fulfilled as I met those expectations. I cooked, but if I was tired or didn't feel like cooking, cooking wasn't happening. I cleaned, but it could wait if I didn't want to. It was a real struggle to measure up to this woman they had expected me to be; I just didn't have that burning passion to be a "great wifey." I wasn't there yet, and I had a lot to learn and needed some grace to get there.

Learning Each Other

In the early stages of many new relationships, you're completely infatuated with your partner. You adore the quirkiest things about them—how they yawn, stand, and blink their eyes. You might even find yourself loving that ugly Eddie Munster "V" on their forehead that distinguishes them from the rest. However, the exposure goes a little deeper when you are under the same roof. You see the real them and might wonder, "What happened?" They don't look as flawless in the morning as they did on those picture-perfect dates, right? You are faced with the real them, pun intended, with no filter on that baby!

Once you get past the brand-newness of dating, the real test comes with a few arguments. You then discover what truly gets on each other's nerves, and those initial infatuations suddenly carry less weight. Even as a married couple! You go from being obsessed with their every move to wanting to punch their head off because they squeeze the toothpaste from the middle rather than the bottom. You're annoyed because they don't dry the dishes before putting them in the cabinet. And you find yourself disgusted with the filthy socks in every corner of your house. Ah, love—it's a rollercoaster.

In our case, we were transitioning from a couple in the early stages of dating to a couple living a married lifestyle, all at the same time. I wasn't fully prepared to accept someone else's way of living apart from mine. As we learned more about each other, it became clear that we were nothing alike. He had his way of doing things, and I had mine. I had convinced myself that we had a lot in common, and I found that we were opposites. Suddenly, that saying that repeats as "opposites attract" didn't seem to apply to us.

Our personalities were like night and day. He was quiet and shy, while I was loud and ready to explore the world. I loved to laugh and was funny, and he didn't have much of a sense of humor; his jokes often fell into the categories of either being a bit coarse or just plain corny, and I was neither.

We didn't even see eye to eye when it came to faith, which complicated our already non-traditional relationship even more. He came from a wishy-washy Catholic background, and I was raised in a *Raja-tabla*, fire-filled, Pentecostal church, where we followed every instruction to the letter. Our differences were obvious on so many scales. Even our socializing styles were also very different. He was content with having just one friend, working, and then coming home to relax, watch a show, and drink a beer. It might sound like a mature way of life to some, but that's not what I wanted.

Keep in mind that I was in my late teens and had just cut the cord with my parents. I wanted to experience the party scene, try new things, and embrace free living. While Jayce never openly objected to my desire for adventure, it made sense why he didn't want to be a part of it. He had already done everything I wanted to experience as a young girl.

We had many more differences that extended past our personalities and perspectives. I realized this when I was trying to complete simple life tasks like enrolling in school and opening a bank account without a guardian. Because of my age, these things were a hassle for me, while they were a breeze for him.

When it came to work ethic, he was much like my father—a hard worker. He held down two full-time jobs and rarely took a day off. Meanwhile,

I was ready to call out if I had a rough night's sleep. I struggled with managing the responsibilities of adulthood. I loved the fruit that came out of that harvest of hard work but hated the labor, and I made sure to let it be known. However, I found it true that we were very much alike in character when it came to this one thing: healthy confrontation. We had no idea how to do it well.

He never wanted to engage in disagreements because he felt they would escalate into heated arguments. While my perspective on disagreements was that they were necessary, I also struggled to communicate my differences for fear of being disliked. We could never get to the bottom of anything because of our immaturity. This created tension, and it affected both of us in a way where we would shut down and allow silence to speak for us for days and days on end. Unfortunately, we were not mature enough to take the initiative to address the issues or make amends. We only tackled our problems once we had no choice but to face them head-on. Even then, we often left our conversations unfinished.

A significant part of our issues had to do with those unresolved talks, especially the ones related to the topic of my schooling. I was looking for a quick fix to get school out of the way. This is why I opted to find a program to help me obtain my G.E.D. rather than completing high school through the traditional route. However, things changed once I realized that I still had the chance to experience some of the typical high school milestones that came with memorable celebrations. Going for a G.E.D. meant missing out on things like prom and that special walk across the graduation stage. Deep down, I wanted to have those moments. So, I decided to enroll in a local alternative high school that would allow me to work during the day, go to school at night, finish high school within a year, and still have those things I wanted. Attending this alternative school would make this the sixth high school switch in three states within four years. I knew he wasn't thrilled about this, and it was clear in his attitude.

Another issue was my mother's constant requests for help, which was a pattern. Sometimes, I didn't always have the extra to give. So when I did give, it would stretch our finances thin. As much as I wanted to say no, I couldn't help myself. I was still struggling with "survivor's guilt." I still felt guilty about being okay. I still felt guilty about choosing me. I now know that this was a skewed perception, and I don't think Jayce could've truly understood me unless he had been through this. So, I shouldn't have expected him to feel anything less than burdened and bothered. But I understand how my sacrificial love towards my mom removed healthy boundaries.

Then there was the issue of all issues. This one infuriated me the most—the stories he told me, particularly those involving his so-called female best friend. Every time he mentioned her, it felt like he was reminiscing about a lost love he had given up while settling for me. I couldn't help but feel insecure as he spoke about this girl he once referred to as "The One." The way he recounted his stories about his female best friend made it obvious they had a deep emotional connection beyond friendship. He would dive deep into the details of their inside jokes and the bond they had cultivated over the years. It often left me feeling like I was the second fiddle.

Rather than picking up on all the red flags, I saw it as a challenge to win his heart fully. I knew I should have spoken up and set some boundaries, but I couldn't bring myself to do it. I was just too scared of losing what I had with Jayce. It's unbelievable to think that I was jealous of someone I didn't even know, all because of how Jayce spoke about her. It made me believe he would choose her over me if the opportunity arose. I thought I was strong enough to suppress my feelings and frustrations at the expense of my sanity to keep the peace. This is people-pleasing at its best.

As similar scenarios continued to come my way, resentment continued to build, but the courage to speak did not. I thought, "Relationships must go through things to become stronger." So I waited it out. Looking back, I can see how I handled this situation with shades of my parent's behavior. Dad always made decisions out of fear, Mom always wanted to wait things out no matter how bad they were, and I was beginning to do the same.

Chapter Twelve

Running From God

I had recently started a new job as a packer in a factory. This was quite a change from the type of work I was used to. It was the first time I had a job working a 1st shift, Monday through Friday, with a set schedule from 6:00 am to 2:30 pm. While having set hours was nice, I was not a morning person. But what I really couldn't get over wasn't even the early rise that came with the job. It was the feeling of the cardboard boxes that scraped against each other that would make me grind my teeth. And don't even get me started on the lunchroom that smelled like last year's old dumpster.

I was very young compared to most of my coworkers, which was obvious because of my attitude. I was more passionate about things that most didn't care about, and this was reflected in my ratchet mouth. I sure needed Jesus, but my ratchet mouth? It could have used a good scrubbing and Jesus. And in a place like this, where no one cared about what I deemed right or wrong, my immaturity rubbed these grown folks the wrong way. Let's just say these were my "terrible teen" years. Cheers to growing pains!

I was building my life the way I wanted to during this time. But Jesus, in his goodness and mercy, persistently sought ways to interrupt my agenda despite what I wanted. He always made sure to have me in the company of genuine believers. In every job, every school I attended, and every place I called home, there was always someone who knew the Lord. I always had at least one Christian boss, one Christian coworker, and even a Christian teacher. I could never run away from God even if I tried. He always had true representatives placed in all my transitions. What I mean by "true Christian folks" is that they were the ones who not only professed their faith by mouth but also lived it out with their lives. They were the ones who didn't live with compromise, unlike those who professed Christianity and had no fruit in their lives.

Shortly after I began working at this factory, a new guy showed up on the scene. He was one of those "real believers" shouting it from the rooftops. He lived and breathed the Gospel, a walking billboard for Jesus, never backing down even when people made fun of him. He brought up topics like sin, hell, heaven, forgiveness, and God's love in a way that got everyone's attention. He also didn't sugarcoat things or care to tickle ears.

During lunch breaks, I'd often overhear him asking questions based on the Ten Commandments to help people understand that merely following the law couldn't lead to salvation. He emphasized using the Ten Commandments as a starting point so that people could see that salvation would be unattainable without the sacrifice Jesus made to pay for our sins.

The questions were somewhere along the lines of this: "Have you ever told a lie? Ever stolen something? Have you ever had lustful thoughts about someone else?" So on and so forth. When they said yes, he would ask,

"Then what does that make you?" The big banger that came with this questionnaire was something that sounded like this.

"Well, by your own admission, you've admitted that you are a liar, a thief, an adulterer, and that means you are guilty."

"If you died right now, based off of all the commandments that you have broken, do you think you'd go to Heaven or Hell?"

Some would respond with hell as the answer but quickly follow up with responses like, "Well, I'm a good person, so I'm going to Heaven."

Some would brush off what he said like he was crazy, while others were offended. But for the ones that were convicted, they would acknowledge by their admission that they were a sinner in need of a savior, and just like that, he would present the plan of salvation. Once I heard him doing the same thing to everyone, I knew it would only be a matter of time before he was coming for me, too. I dodged this man as much as I could. Whenever I walked through the warehouse and noticed that the preacher boy was heading my way, I would purposely take another route. If I couldn't avoid him and we had to cross paths, I made sure to say nothing! I wouldn't say hi, bye, cat, dog, nothing! I didn't need him to point out the sins in my life; I was well aware of the kinds of sins I was committing.

I knew that I was a sinner who loved my sins more than God. I just didn't want him to confront me about it, and I certainly didn't want to be held accountable for my actions. I wanted God to leave me alone and let me continue sinning without any consequences. I wanted God's blessing; I wanted His hand. But I wanted a "No strings attached" type of relationship with Him.

Ohhhh, but the holy roller got me! God knew exactly how to use him to get me, too. He didn't catch me in the lunchroom or the packing area, just like he caught everyone else. God knew He had to set me up in a position where running away would not be an option. While I worked at this factory, walking was my transportation to get home. My walks home were a little over an hour. Sometimes, I would get offers for rides, but most times, I declined and walked.

One hot summer day, after an eight-hour shift, as I was exiting the lot on foot, I saw a car slowly pull up beside me. When I looked, it was the preacher boy. In my mind, I'm thinking, "Awww, man, it's you!" He offered me a ride. Typically, I would have said no, but I was tired that day, and as exhausted as I was, I would've said yes to a donkey's back if that was all that was available. I accepted his offer, hoping he would say nothing, but the kid couldn't help himself. I had hoped he would've been intimidated by my stank girl face. Instead, it was like he saw an open invitation for testimony time.

He gave me a little background about himself, his wife, his kids, and how he met the Lord. He asked me many open-ended questions about my life. I was trying to be careful because I knew he would take advantage of this opportunity to preach to me. Either way, I ended up putting my foot in my mouth. In conversation, I spewed out a mishmash of the little scripture I could remember as I tried my best to sound as close to a believer as possible. Little did I know that my responses put the hook right into my mouth, and he immediately picked up on the skit. Did I forget to mention that I told this Christian man that I was living with my boyfriend?

He found a spot in the conversation and slipped in that questionnaire he gave everyone at work. The one I tried so hard to avoid. I didn't know it then, but that questionnaire is part of a curriculum called "The Way Of The Master." This is a simple step-by-step course created by an evangelist to help other evangelists preach the Gospel. He also took advantage of this moment to address that little fun fact I decided to share about living with my boyfriend.

He gently slapped me up, referencing 2 Corinthians 6:14, and said, "You know you are unequally yoked, right?"

The look on my face was like, "What?" I began defending why living in sin with Jayce was okay. I really believed that God would allow me to live out this sin so that he could use me to change Jayce's heart toward Him. The preacher boy quickly corrected my thought process and said,

"God will never put you in a situation that will cause you to sin against Him to bring someone into the kingdom."

I got defensive and tried to back up my emotional theory with my limited knowledge of scripture. I had wished I had the guts to open the car door and roll right out. He then shared what he believed was an incredible plan for my life, even throwing in the classic John 3:16 spiel right before I got home. But by then, I was so wrapped up in my offense that I tuned him out halfway through the car ride. Sometimes, no matter how much you try to sugarcoat something, the truth will hurt if you are convinced your lie is true. And that was me.

I was delusional. Confident that this lie was my truth. But this guy corrected me with truth, wrapped in love. He didn't self-righteously preach or argue with me back and forth to prove a point. Instead, he just shared the living word of God, and his motive was to bring Jesus, not boost his ego.

We made it to my house and I tried my best to exit the car without letting my frustration show on my face, but I was mad! Now, here is the thing: Just because I didn't accept Jesus as my savior that day in the car didn't mean seeds weren't planted. He might not have known, and maybe he never will, but that moment left a lasting mark on me.

As I made my way to my apartment, I felt guilty about the life I was living. I wanted to repent, but it wasn't that easy for me. My verbal repentance would have only been the first step in cleaning house in my life. The next step would've been letting go of everything that wasn't aligned with God's will, including my relationship with Jayce. I just knew that if and when I said yes to Jesus, Jayce wouldn't have been a part of that. And I just wasn't ready to go there yet.

Jayce didn't really have a church background. So, he wouldn't have comprehended what committing to Jesus meant. And it's not just about what that commitment would've required of me but also what it would've demanded of us both. He didn't know the Holy Spirit, and he mocked the faith. He was set on believing that a life devoted to God was for "religious fanatics." He had no desire to alter his beliefs or lifestyle to surrender to a

Jesus that, to him, wasn't real. I began to think about what type of friction this would bring, and it challenged me to reflect on what exactly I was building here. We didn't have any children then, but what if that ended up being in the cards? And having kids was a real possibility. Although I was only considering committing my life to God, I knew that bringing kids onto the scene would've changed the game. I would have never been able to withhold Biblical Jesus from them. This made me wonder if I could have a life with Christ and Jayce. Or would I eventually have to choose between them? I knew the answers to these questions, even though I wasn't eager to know them. I certainly didn't have the guts to end our relationship in the name of God. Instead, I held onto the hope that somehow, God would step in and make things right, and I would get everything that I wanted.

Chapter Thirteen

Confirmed

Going to college was not on the agenda. I had only prepared for what I considered important, like a driver's license, a car, and a decent job with decent pay to get by. Compared to where I was just a few years ago, I was winning! I had a job, paid rent, and the lights were on. I had more stability in my life than I had in the last five years all together. All this was good, but it didn't feel like it was enough anymore.

I often compared my accomplishments to Jayce's and felt inadequate. He had an education and trades under his belt. He had two great jobs that paid him what he was worth. He was very established, and I felt ashamed about not achieving even the most basic things he had done. I was a high school dropout with a G.E.D., working a minimum-wage part-time job; I had no driver's license, savings account, or degrees. In my eyes, he made us great, and I added nothing to that. Although it was clear that he had a head start due to his age and experiences, I never acknowledged that he had an advantage. As an eighteen-year-old girl trying to find her way in the world, I was so hard on myself. I completely overlooked the fact that I was young. I failed to see that even with all my disadvantages, I was exactly where I should have been.

I had my eye on a Cosmetology school conveniently within walking distance from where I lived. I had often walked past this school and wondered what it could have looked like for me if I had pursued a career in cosmetology. One day, I finally got the courage to find out. I called and made an appointment, and before I knew it, I was enrolled in school. I was so excited about this venture and ready to share it with whoever would listen. I was proud of myself for taking risks and daring to chase a dream. It seemed like the road was paved for this, too, because there wasn't much I needed to rearrange to start school. Except, there was one thing that I failed to do. I failed to guard my heart. I allowed the opinions of others to kill my dreams.

You have given someone too much power when you allow their feelings and opinions to dictate your life decisions. That type of power gives people the ability to give your dreams life, or it can give them the power to abort them. You have to be careful who you give that type of power to because dream abortion is a real thing. It's interesting how the journey of giving up on your dreams often starts with comments like, "Why would you even want to do that? It doesn't seem like there's a future in that!" Or it can sound like, "That's never going to work!"

Sadly, because of my insecurities, I let these remarks persuade me into believing that failure was inevitable. Ironically enough, failure is unavoidable. But failure does not have to be the end result. You can look at failure as the comma that comes before success. I didn't even give myself a chance before I allowed someone else's disapproval to extinguish my motivation, and I was on the phone canceling the contract. And this didn't happen once or twice but several times.

Shortly after this failed endeavor, I shifted gears and pursued what I believed was a reputable career. I reached out to a local college that offered an L.P.N. (Licensed Practical Nurse) program. Jayce accompanied me to the school to apply for the basic entry exam. Walking into that building, I felt like a champion, and the confidence that welled up in me gave me hope for the future I had always wanted. Just thinking about the future I could have had already made me feel like I was somebody.

I don't know if my past experiences with school and self-discipline influenced Jayce's response to my excitement, but his reaction was not what I wanted to hear or see. Frustrated, he asked, "Are you sure this is what you want?" If he only knew how much courage it took to apply to this program. Sure, I wanted this for me, but I wanted this for us too. I wanted Jayce to feel proud introducing me as someone with status rather than just a sales associate stuck at a dead-end job. Things took an unexpected turn, as what was supposed to be a moment of celebration turned into a mortifying experience that I will never forget.

As requested, I went to the school to pick up the results from the basic entry exam. Upon arrival, the program director asked to see me in her office. She asked me to take a seat. As I sat down, I noticed her shaking her head as she looked at my test scores.

"I mean, did you even study? With scores like these, there's no way you can get into a nursing program!" she said.

I must have been one of the worst she had ever seen. She recommended that if I wanted to return and retake the test, I should hire a tutor and study hard. But after what was said, along with the backhanded opinions, I never wanted to put myself in a position where I would allow myself to feel that stupid again. To cope with the disappointment, I abandoned the desire to dream and reverted to what I knew. I picked up a second job, and I worked.

A Whole New World

I befriended a girl I met while working my part-time night job. We had a lot in common, making our relationship feel more organic. We became incredibly close rather quickly. She became the person I vented to about my relationship, my ongoing family affairs, and all the things that burdened me. She did the same with me. What I admired most about her was how she'd bravely say, "I've been through that too!" She never pretended to have it all together when she didn't. She was transparent, fearless, and bold, and I aspired to be a little like her.

But here's where things got tricky—she was single, and I wasn't. And we all know what comes with a single life. It's all about doing your own thing, making decisions based solely on your needs and wants, and not having to answer to anyone. I wasn't controlled, but I was in a committed relationship, and that meant that there were some restrictions on my end.

Given my age and lack of life experiences, it was only a matter of time before I wanted to take adult freedom to another level. As I mentioned before, Jayce had already done everything I wanted to do. So, even if I wanted to live this out with him, he was uninterested.

One night, my friend invited me to an eighteen-and-over club. Since all we had where I lived were pubs, and I didn't meet the age requirement, I quickly said yes. Here's where it gets interesting—the club my friend invited me to wasn't a dance club. It was a gentlemen's club, which is a huge difference from a nightclub.

We arrived at the club, and as I approached the door, I handed over my ID to the bouncer. After a quick check, I paid the entry fee, received a wristband, and stepped inside. I found a whole new world beyond those doors. The place was filled with booming music, glowing teeth, women dressed in lingerie with loads of cash, and I'm sure you have enough imagery of what the rest could've looked like. I tried my best to act like I wasn't fazed by it all, but I couldn't help but wonder how everyone maintained such a nonchalant attitude in such a promiscuous environment. Everyone there appeared to be having a good time, and I did my best to mirror their mood, trying to hide the fact that it was my first time there. Little did I know that this would not be the first or last time I would enter this place.

I began to use this space to unwind and chill, just like I had seen others do so casually. I'd head out on a Friday night and often wouldn't return home until about three in the morning. The next day, I'd go to work and do it all over again, or any other day, I was free to do so. Interestingly, I often found myself facing questions about my sexuality because of my frequent visits to the gentlemen's club. Initially, my frequent visits were more of a substitution for the typical nightclub experience I couldn't access yet—or so I believed.

Regardless of my intentions, this became another opportunity for satan to have a free hand in my life. And we all know how satan plays this game. He will make the most of every opportunity that comes, and he never does it with anything new; instead, he often capitalizes on what's already there, especially things introduced through trauma.

My introduction to same-sex attraction was not birthed in a place like this. Rather, it was introduced during childhood. I believed I was in control of my thoughts, body, and choices; therefore, there was no way that an environment like this would've "turned me out," as they would say. I never would have thought that a place like this would ever alter my beliefs on sexuality. But if I had no relationship with the Holy Spirit, who would be the one to help me with such enticements?

My New World

The friend who took me to the gentlemen's club was once an exotic dancer. When she filled me in on how much money you could rack up doing this, I quickly began to consider it. She wanted to get back into it for the same reasons I thought about starting—the money. We're talking about making more cash in part-time hours at a good club than folks who have college degrees make working their dream job.

She was bold and carefree about this move, and I admired that! Her mantra was, "If you're not paying my bills, I don't care what you have to say!" Well, that's the PG version. But as much as I longed to embody her bold and carefree spirit, I couldn't apply that same attitude to this situation—again, because I was in a relationship.

As I calculated every move in my head, I envisioned what the next two years of my life would look like with a bold move like this. I could work three to four nights a week, double my income, pay off loans while attending school, and finally obtain everything I needed to establish myself. This fast money could have quickly sorted life out in no time. It seemed like a no-brainer. In my mind, it was a simple method, with a small sacrifice to make, and I would owe no one anything in the process.

Jayce was well aware of what my friend once did for a living and was openly involved in some of our chats about this matter. Surprisingly, he never had anything negative to say. If anything, he gave off the impression of respecting the hustle, even amongst those involved in relationships.

Based on his response to this topic and how I had been thinking about moving forward, I began sparking up conversations with him about the possibility of becoming a dancer. At first, it was a mixed bag, but then he left the ball in my court.

As I continue to tell my story, please keep in mind that many of the thoughts I share related to the events in my life were before I became a believer. I only share my story and thoughts in raw detail because so many think just like this and don't detect the anti-God agenda in it.

Jayce and I finally discussed what I viewed as an opportunity. In that same week, I auditioned at the club and immediately began working. Working at the club felt like I was going to a wild party every night, except I was sober and there to work. Not having a lick of alcohol in me allowed my consciousness to get to me.

"Why am I here? I shouldn't be here! What if someone I know walks in? What if Jayce decides to leave me because of this job?"

These were the thoughts that were running through my mind. But my misdirected determination shoved those unwelcome thoughts into the recesses of my mind. That determination drove me to focus more on the eventual outcome of what I considered to be a sacrifice rather than the part of the job that felt degrading.

Having to be flirtatious and promiscuous was part of the job, and it was something I wasn't comfortable with. You would've never found me wearing even a bathing suit in public without fidgeting and trying to stretch fabric where it would not stretch. I was young, inexperienced, and scared. Working with women who were not only seasoned dancers but also models with a wealth of experience in the game really heightened that insecurity. I couldn't see how a tiny nineteen-year-old gal like myself would have been able to keep up and compete with these seasoned pros, let alone make the kind of money they made.

The girls could see my insecurity, and they quickly offered strategies. They cheered me on, reassuring me that I would improve over time, that I shouldn't worry too much about cash flow, and that clientele and cash flow would eventually come with consistency. Once I locked in some of those strategies and grew more confident, the money started rolling in, and...I fell in love with the fast money. I fell in love with the attention, the thought of being desired, and the false recognition—although what I received wasn't genuine, anything resembling approval was good enough for me.

In an environment such as this one, where fantasies were created for many, I was able to create the illusion of the person I truly wanted to be. I gave myself a new name, a different age, and a higher social status. I spun the tale of a woman with goals, security, confidence, and finesse—the kind of woman I believed was a top-notch woman. I never realized that I enjoyed weaving these fictional stories together about myself because, deep down, I hated who I really was.

Confirmed

It was pretty common to spot some of the girl's significant others at the club on busy weekend nights. I often wondered how they pulled it off without getting into arguments or succumbing to feelings of jealousy. To avoid some of the common issues with this line of work and condition Jayce and me to adapt better, I decided to invite Jayce, too. I aimed to make this career move feel as normal as possible so that we could achieve *our* goals: his security within our relationship and the life I yearned for.

When Jayce arrived at the club that Saturday night, I greeted him as I would have in any other place. I introduced him to some of the girls I had befriended as well. He grabbed a drink, found a seat, and I went to work. *Le tiré un ojo por si acaso.-* I kept a close eye on him, just in case. I looked away for what felt like a second, and when I looked back, I was shocked to find him interacting with one of the dancers in a manner I had not expected.

And that's not even the worst part of it! He knew this girl outside of the club scene by name, attached with a phone number. This was not the first time this had happened, and it was way before this job was brought to the table. I was very bothered by what I saw, but I felt like I had no right to judge him because of what I was doing. But it didn't change how I felt.

That night, we argued about what I witnessed and how he felt about this job. When all was said and done, I ended up quitting the club. Even though I wanted to not care about what this job could cost me, I couldn't help but care about what was left of us. This debacle only added to the plethora of issues we encountered.

All of this took place right before the Thanksgiving Holiday, and I felt like I needed a small break. So I decided to take a trip back home to visit my mom. But something strange happened during that Thanksgiving getaway. I unexpectedly crossed paths with a family member *we* the family considered the "creepy family member." This family member was known for sensing things before they happened and reading people accurately. I had always avoided this person, and I tried to do the same this time, but they got me.

Our eyes met as I sat by a window at my relative's home. I just knew that they were about to tell me something I didn't want to hear. Internally, I was screaming in Spanish, *"Tierra, trágame."* – This means swallow me up ground. With their eyes peering into what felt like my soul, he said to me in Spanish, *"¿Sabes algo? Tú no vas a durar mucho tiempo con ese muchachito."* Which translates to "You want to know something? You're not going to last too long with that kid." Their words felt like someone had tied a rock around my neck and just threw me into the ocean to sink. It was as if they had confirmed what I had been sensing for a long time. Without giving it much thought, I said, "I already know that."

As I left that Thanksgiving getaway, I didn't feel particularly thankful and was left with the anticipation of what lay ahead.

Confirmed Part II

In the following months, Jayce made a career change that required him to undergo extensive training. This new job also had a longer commute, forcing him to leave home earlier. However, I couldn't help but notice that he was leaving much earlier than he needed. When questioned about it, he justified his early departure by emphasizing the importance of punctuality. That didn't concern me as much as what came with it. What raised eyebrows was that along with this sudden schedule change, he was sending and receiving constant text messages at all hours of the day and night that were not from me. This had actually been going on for a while, even before I began to notice. My suspicions were confirmed with a review of our paper cell phone bill. When I confronted him about these messages, he admitted they were from another woman. However, he reassured me that their communication was strictly work-related.

The thought that he might be cheating felt like a real possibility. And it stressed me out! When I say that I was stressed, *hmmmm*, I was stressed. I went to bed anxious, woke up angry and worried, had many restless nights with no peace, smoking nearly two packs of cigarettes a day, even with borderline pneumonia. I couldn't believe we were only three years in, and this was all that was left.

I knew that things were different between us. I could sense that we were growing apart and wanted different things. To make matters worse, if this relationship had ended, as I was sure it would, I was completely unprepared for what would come next. I didn't have a stable job, I had no savings to fall back on, and the apartment was under his name. If we ended, then I would have to start over. If I couldn't get myself together quickly, I would have to go and live with my mom, and that was the last thing I wanted to do. Moving in with Mom wasn't necessarily a bad thing; I just felt like I had nothing to go back to. With my mom still struggling, I felt guilty about trying to rebuild my life on her limited resources.

Shortly after suspicions arose about that woman from his job, Jayce transitioned to another job. With this transition, we found ourselves in a financial rut. Due to this, our cell phones were shut down. But I had a prepaid phone that I stashed away for emergencies. This situation definitely qualified as one since he was working farther away. One day, I woke up with this overwhelming sense of heaviness, heavier than most days. This weight was tied to what I can only describe as a premonition of what I was about to uncover.

I had a light bulb moment while trying to unpack what I was sensing. I remembered the prepaid phone I had given him a while back and planned to go through it. When I asked for the phone, he handed it over without fuss, hesitation, or resistance. For a moment, I felt guilty about my suspicion. Maybe I was trying too hard to find something that didn't exist. But that inkling wasn't going away, and I was not about to let that *"ay bendito"*- get in the way. I didn't trust him, and that lack of resistance easily could have been a part of the act. As I took that phone and sat on the back porch that late summer afternoon, I was determined to uncover the truth.

I took a deep breath, lit a cigarette, and began my investigation. I meticulously went through every contact in the phonebook, every call and every call received. I combed through every text message on that phone, sent, received, and deleted. I didn't find anything that was flat-out considered cheating. Still, I didn't feel the need to stop searching. I even went through the internet history to see if there were any strange sites that he had visited and found nothing. I paused and thought to myself, "Girl, you're bugging! Maybe there's nothing serious going on? Maybe it's just flirting and nothing more. You can get over that, right?"

Nonetheless, I kept looking through the phone, desperately determined to find something that would alleviate my growing anxiety and kill the suspicion. I decided to search through all of the apps as my last attempt. I would completely give up the suspicion if I didn't find anything. Specifically, I began searching through the chat line apps that I didn't even know existed. Strangely, these apps were all activated, and I certainly hadn't been the one who activated them. All of these chatlines required passwords, and I don't know how in the world I managed to figure out all the passwords to every account he had created with no hassle, but I did.

What I saw next made my jaw drop. It was exactly what I had suspected all along, and it had been going on for quite some time, just as I feared it had. He had been conversing with multiple girls simultaneously, both local and from his hometown. Clearly, these weren't innocent hellos. But to think that for a split second, I almost gave up the suspicion because I felt bad.

Running into this information made it difficult to keep my composure. I was unsure of what my reaction should have been. Unable to control my rising anger, I began reading the messages I had found out loud, dripping with sarcasm. His reaction was priceless. He sprung up from that futon like he was Jack in the Box. He rushed toward me, attempting to come up with a phony explanation for the evidence that had been uncovered. But I knew he had sent those messages because I recognized the language and the expressions he used. In a bold move, I contacted one of the mains he had been communicating with. I called her from the prepaid phone, and when she realized what was happening, she spilled the beans.

When I tell you that this girl put him on blast, *shawty put him on blast!* She started sharing personal information about him that was just too accurate to be a coincidence. How could she have known these things? He was left speechless, stuttering, and struggling to connect his thoughts. I couldn't believe he was still trying to come up with lies to cover it up. Considering how things had been between us, I would have at least expected him to tell me the truth.

I used to be the type who judgmentally told people what to do in various situations I had never experienced. Now, here I was, confronted with the same problem I judged so many for and didn't know what to do. At that moment, I empathized with anyone I had once labeled foolish. In moments of intense pressure, you draw blanks. You're not always sure of the appropriate response.

I, too, was unprepared to deliver the kind of proud, loud, and witty "aha, I caught you" speech I had envisioned. Part of me wanted to lash out and say everything I despised about him to hurt him in return, and then another part of me wanted to hide under a rock because my worst fear had come.

For the next several weeks, I hated his guts and let it be known with all my spiteful actions and comebacks. Since we had broken up after this huge fight, I was now technically single, and I could do whatever I wanted, and he could say, "*NADA!*" I would come and go whenever I pleased, with whomever I pleased, and I was in and out of the house at all hours of the night. All I was doing was hanging out at a friend's house, but I wanted him to wonder. I wanted him to hurt the way I was hurting. There was nothing else I could do to make him suffer other than to make him wonder. But I had also wondered if this was really the end of us.

There is a saying in Spanish that says, *"Donde hubo fuego, cenizas hay."* Wherever there was a fire, ashes will be found. But why was I hoping to find a spark in something that was already snuffed out? D esperation speaks loudly in low moments, finding ways to whisper sweet, delusional lies to bring you false comfort. My desire to reignite what was lost stemmed from a need for comfort, familiarity, and the fear of navigating something new rather than a genuine desire to work things out for the sake of love.

Remember, he was all I had ever known in the realm of "relationships." He was the only person I had allowed to come that close to my heart. So, of course, I had put all my trust in this man, believing he would make me whole. Of course, I was sure this relationship would fill all the voids in my life. But if I had the knowledge and wisdom I have now, I would tell myself that it wasn't his job to complete me, nor was it his job to provide me with the sense of identity I was desperately searching for. I would alleviate my heartache by reminding myself that he was a man, nothing more than an imperfect, flawed man who was just as broken as I was.

These emotional highs and lows were closely tied to the sentiment of grief. As we know, grief isn't just tied to the mourning of a physical death; grief is attached to any form of death. The thing that makes grief so difficult to process is that you can't rush it. You simply must allow yourself to feel and heal through it. I had never been through anything like this before, and I didn't realize how hard healing really was.

I didn't know what to measure these sentiments against. What were the right feelings I was supposed to feel? How angry was too angry? How sad was too sad? If I were to move on, how fast was too fast? There were so many questions, few clear answers, and I didn't know how and where to find them.

Chapter Fourteen

A Dark Beginning

As a kid, I don't remember ever being brave about anything. I feared just about everything, from heights and bugs, to rain, possible floods, and thunderstorms. My list of fears always surpassed the list of things I had ever conquered. Fear was engraved in my DNA. I believe that it came in first through my dad, then religion. Both believed that enforcing strict rules and setting impossibly high standards was the only way to make someone obedient. But none of these "laws" established by my dad or religion made me more compliant. Instead, they pushed me further away, leaving me frustrated and rebellious towards both my earthly father and God.

Let me emphasize on this. There is a healthy fear of the Lord. It's not about being scared or terrified of Him, though it can be terrifying for some. Rather, it's about recognizing His Divinity, Greatness, Holiness,

Majesty, and reverencing Him as God Almighty. Fearing the Lord involves acknowledging His sovereignty and limitless power. It's the realization that God is all-knowing, Omnipotent, and Omniscient. We must accept and acknowledge that He is not our equal and is not subject to our limited understanding of all things. He is superior, and comprehending all these grand attributes should lead us to a place of awe and wonder. The fear of the Lord should inspire us to live in a manner that aligns with His character and principles.

After the breakup, I realized that I had unhealthy fears beyond God and my father. Identifying this was a positive step, but this realization didn't necessarily lead me to the kind of freedom I'm sure God would have wanted for me. Whether I knew that the type of freedom I pursued was the type of freedom God wanted for me, I was determined to break through every boundary placed by religion, man, and tradition and bust through every glass ceiling. Beginning with my introduction to singlehood and independence.

Since my only experience of being single and free was like... never! It tells you how much I really knew about being single. I didn't even know how to flirt. In fact I was so inexperienced with singleness that I didn't even know what I was attracted to. I didn't know if I liked husky guys. I didn't know if I only liked tall, skinny guys. I didn't know what I was attracted to as far as personality. I only knew what I didn't like because of the relationship I just got out of.

Facing this emerging part of my life felt scary and intimidating, but embracing singleness was less painful than I had imagined. Singleness brought more benefits than the disadvantages I had expected.

For one, I had priceless peace and no longer had anything to argue about. For two, the need to ask for explanations or begin investigations because of suspicions was gone. If I could compare the feeling to anything relatable, it would be like working at a job you wanted to quit, and you stayed there because you were afraid to take the risk of leaving. But then, when you finally gain the courage to quit, you realize all the peace you missed out on and wonder why you didn't quit sooner. Yes! Exactly! I know you felt that!

Now that I was single single, I wanted to become more confident. I began doing what I imagined confident people would do: wear what you want, say what's on your mind, and make the world believe you are all that and a bag of chips. I sure dated myself with that comment. I noticed more attraction towards this "confidence" that I was walking out versus that mean girl, victimized, entitled attitude I had before. I expected to attract attention. However, this was not a healthy form of confidence because this confidence was no longer about self-improvement. Instead, this distorted confidence was focused on leveraging the attention to manipulate and charm others into giving me what I wanted.

We know that a real confident person will not change how they feel about themselves because they are not validated by others. No matter what you think, say, or feel, they are who they are, and they are not easily moved by anyone's opinion. And even though that is who I had dreamed of becoming, I was so far from that!

A short time after Jayce and I broke up, I was hanging out at a friend's house. My friend's daughter was hanging out with a few of her friends while I visited. They all knew I could sing and kept insisting that I sing.

I decided to sing a little something something. Meanwhile, one of the girls here pulled out their phone out and started recording me. Without me knowing, they shared this video with several people. Through a series of connections, one of the people who saw the footage convinced my friend's daughter, who knew where I lived, to plan an unexpected visit to my apartment with them.

If you knew me personally back then, I was pretty private regarding certain things. For example, if you were outside my circle of friends, it would not be okay to show up at my house unannounced. Period! Coincidently, the same day Jayce was moving out of the apartment, there was an unexpected knock on my door. While I could have chosen not to answer, curiosity got the best of me. To my surprise, it was my friend's daughter, the same one I had been hanging out with that day I was recorded. And she wasn't alone. She was with some random girl I had never seen in my life.

I awkwardly allowed them to come in. "*Wow, es que esta tipa es bien atrevida*!" I thought, "Wow, this chick is very daring." It probably would have been wise to tell her that her unexpected visit was very bad timing, not to mention that she brought some random person to my place. Still, I allowed them to come in and tried my best to host them while not making things so awkward. The random girl takes a seat in my living room, and my friend's daughter gives me a short, dry introduction of who that random girl was. I then ask, "What brings you around?" Her response was suspicious, to say the least. "Just visiting." She said. She never "just visited" if her mom wasn't with her. This immediately raised a red flag. Without a shadow of a doubt, there was an ulterior motive behind this "random visit."

Next, Jayce comes out of the bedroom with some of his belongings in a box. My friend's daughter asks, confused, "Y'all moving out?" I chuckle, "Nah, he's moving out." Their faces look like they want to ask some more. So, before they could ask anything, I cut straight to the chase: "We're not together anymore."

While the random girl went to use my bathroom, my friend's daughter rushed over to tell me something. She began whispering in her broken Spanish as she looked back to make sure the random girl couldn't overhear. "*Ella te gusta!*" "She likes you!" she said. My initial annoyance at their abrupt visit quickly turned into a flattering moment. It all made sense now—the girl was there because she was interested in me.

Knowing she went out of her way to meet me because she was attracted to me boosted my confidence. It made me feel like I hit another rank on the hot girl list because I was not only wanted by men but now I was wanted by women, too. While basking in self-glory, the random girl comes out of the bathroom, and shortly after, they both leave. Do you think I was going to keep this to myself? Of course not! I told Jayce exactly why she was there. I wanted to provoke jealousy in him. That abrupt visit was a quick face-to-face encounter for that random girl's satisfaction, a boost to my ego, but I was going to use it as a jab at Jayce. Believe it or not, this was not the last of this random girl.

She began to come around more often. Perhaps her awareness that Jayce was out of the picture gave her some hope. It must have given her more than just hope because homegirl was in it to win it! She was persistent and consistent, but I was unbothered by it. I felt secure in my sexuality, and I saw her attempts as harmless. As long as she remained respectful and never crossed that line, I was okay with her still coming around. She posed no threat.

The "limited access" I gave her allowed her enough leeway to get comfortable enough to make a move. She was attentive to every detail that mattered to me and noted everything I liked, loved, and hated. She would make thoughtful gestures, like surprising me with lunch and dinner tailored to my preferences, which she had picked up on without me telling her. She would volunteer to take me to run all my errands. She took care of me when I got sick. She even sat back and watched me make her second-best next to someone who didn't even try as hard as she did. And even that didn't make her go away. If anything, she just tried harder rather than retracting. All of the things she did began to make me see her in a different light.

As I continued to give her space in my life, she took advantage of every opportunity to try and help me see what she saw. She didn't see homosexuality as anything sinful or lustful. She simplified her lifestyle with a question, "Do you want to be happy?" That statement validated her choices and actions. According to her theory, I should've pursued whatever I desired in the name of happiness.

Her appearance was what they would call "A stud." She had long hair, and very delicate feminine features, making her look more like a pretty boy rather than some John Deer-looking butch I was accustomed to seeing. Because I was starting to become attracted to this "pretty boy "look she became even more appealing to my eye. It allowed me to overlook that she was a woman underneath it all. "This wasn't supposed to happen." I thought.

Why was it that her being a woman suddenly was not an issue anymore? Could it have been that all the experiences I had, from the trauma of my innocence being stolen to the lustful atmospheres I put myself in, helped me to overlook the facts? Or that I received encouragement and validation from society and my inner circle of friends that encouraged me to be more open-minded about my sexuality? The answer is all of the above and some.

It felt like she was giving me everything I needed without any resistance and without me having to request it. Everything that felt like protection, validation, affirmation, acceptance, love, kindness, gentleness, patience, adventure, compassion, and more. Although it came through a counterfeit source, it felt like a pretty, vibrant, colorful gift that I was excited to receive, even if it came straight from satan himself.

I was convinced that I wouldn't go beyond experimentation if I chose to pursue this relationship further. I had absolutely no intentions of it evolving into anything more than that. But how can one set stipulations on sin that is out to rule you? In time, it ruled me as I made room for it to do so. And it all started with a small peck on the lips. Then those pecks became more frequent, and then came the hand-holding in public, giving her more access to me and making this thing we had going on feel more normal.

Giving her that access made it easier for her to convince me to go all the way. It was like dealing with a salesperson who pitched their product as if it came with a 100 percent money-back guarantee. "Let me do it one time, and I won't ever ask you again," she'd say each time it was brought up. Each time, I grew more convinced than the last and more boldness to just to do it. Not long after these small but consistent compromises, I finally gave in! I succumbed to my urges. I chose to go against everything I had ever been told not to do, against what I believed I had enough self-control to avoid.

At nineteen years old, I had my first sexual encounter with someone of the same sex. I was waiting for a lightning bolt to come out of the sky and strike me dead. Or for a car to hit me on my way out of the house as a form of punishment. I could hear my mom's voice in my head, repeating a phrase she often said in Spanish: "*Tú sigues jugando con Dios. A Dios no se le puede engañar!*" "You keep playing with God! You can't fool God."

At that moment, all my feelings, beliefs, and values were a jumbled mess as I had done what I remember the church calling an abomination; I had done the most detestable thing in the sight of God. I seriously questioned everything I had ever been taught about the Bible and this specific sin as my eyes had been opened. I was attracted to the very thing I was told God hated.

Section 5

Chapter Fifteen

Moving On

Jayce signed over the apartment, and this became the perfect opportunity for a fresh start. However, bit by bit, all of my goals and responsibilities were swapped out for a few "YOLO" (*You Only Live Once*) moments. I wanted to do things my way, at my own pace, and on my terms. That mindset caused things to spiral quickly, leading to a major downgrade in who I was. I went from being a hardworking go-getter to someone just drifting through life, jobless, and always seeking the next high. I began hanging out with the wrong crowd, making bad choices, and burning several bridges along the way. The consequences of my choices were irreversible, and it became clear that it was time for me to take Mom up on her offer and stay with her for a while.

When I decided to leave, I didn't consider how this would affect the relationship between this girl and me. But I knew one thing: it was time to tell her the ride was over. As you probably suspected, she wasn't too happy about this change. Shockingly, she didn't change with me after I told her. She continued to be there for me for the remainder of the time, just as she had been there for me since we met. I thought that because I clearly outlined the terms of our relationship, our agreement would serve as the boundary in preventing any interference between what we had and our lives outside of this flame. This gave me the green light to ask this girl to drive me to my mother's house.

In light of this, returning to Mom's house and starting over as a young adult couldn't have been harder than navigating life on my own states away. I was against this move for a while. But, I never stopped to consider all the resources I would've needed to get back on my feet. Moving to a city where essentials like medical benefits, transportation, and job opportunities were easily accessible was probably one of the main reasons I should have made this move sooner."

However, there was a downside to this move. There would be a shift in my comfort level. I would go from having my own apartment to living on the couch. I would transition from a quiet space to a home filled with loud kids and restrictions. But I believed the benefits outweighed the downsides, and the chances of becoming homeless were slim to none. This move would finally give me a moment to just... breathe.

My "friend" and I finally arrived at my mom's house after a long, exhausting six-hour drive. As we went over every speed bump, it forced us to drive slower than normal, giving my friend a moment to scope out the surroundings. She became a little tense as she realized what we were driving into. We were in the projects, and this was the hood. Where we came from looked nothing like what we were driving through.

We parked the car, and my mom was already waiting at the door. You could hear her excitement through her loud, joyful Puerto Rican voice as she shouted, "Hey, girl! "As my "friend" and I got closer to my mother's apartment, I saw the shift in Mom's face. It went from "I'm so glad you're here!" to "*¿Quién es esa tipa??*" Which means, "Who is that chick?" First, let me just say that my so-called "friend" looked different. As I mentioned earlier, she was a stud. This was no big deal for many people in my generation; we embraced diversity without assumption. But my mom was old-school and churchy. So, I expected her to look at her a little sideways.

After the awkward hug at the door, we walked in. I wasted no time introducing my friend to everyone. I did this before any questions could pop up about who this new face was and why she was with me. I almost felt like I was re-introducing myself too. It had been so long since I had seen my family that the first thing I did after the introduction was give my siblings lots of hugs and kisses. I also met my new baby brother, who was just a month old. Despite everything that had been happening in my life and all the struggles I had been facing, this was a moment where I internally paused to soak it all in. I was always the girl who attended other people's family gatherings because I didn't have a family of my own. And in that moment, I felt like I belonged. Although we weren't close, I was reminded I had a family.

That blissful moment was quickly interrupted as I saw my mom approaching me with that look. It was that look that could kill. I knew she had something to say regarding my "friend" who came with me. I figured my mom would give me time to settle in before she began probing. And she gave me some time.... something around twenty-odd minutes before she *HAD* to clarify her statement.

She didn't care that we just came from a six-hour ride. She pulled me aside and said, "*Este... ¿Ella se va a ir, o no?*" Which meant, "Ummm, is she leaving or not?" I responded, "Mom, she just drove six hours to bring me here; can she rest?" She responded again in Spanish, "*Pues ella no se puede quedar aquí mucho tiempo. ¿Cuándo se va a ir?*"-"Well, she can't stay here for long; when will she leave?" To keep her silent for a bit, I told her my friend would be gone by the end of the weekend. Even that was already taking it too far. But that response was good enough to keep her calm for a little while.

I recall being outside on my mom's porch hanging out, kee-keeing and ha-hahing while casually making plans with my "friend" like she was on a mini vacay in the hood. My mom quickly interrupted me to remind me of the terms and conditions of our agreement. She also took advantage of this to slide in a comment about my noticeable behavior. I knew she had recognized that I was not the same girl who left her house over three years ago. And she was right. I wasn't.

So much happened, not just to me but to us. I loved my mother, but I was equally frustrated with her, and because of our history, our relationship had been fractured. I believed that the only way we could heal and even consider having a healthy relationship was for me to have the opportunity to release my unfiltered truth. But I didn't think my mom could handle that. I now know that even if I had been given the opportunity to express my truth, I lacked the self-control to articulate my feelings without anger. I made peace with accepting that the closest thing I would get to closure would be found in silence, and our issues would never be dealt with. I came to terms with the fact that our relationship would be what it was and I would just have to take this thorn to the grave.

As I grew into a young adult, not only did my behavior change, but I developed some habits that my mom was not too fond of. Even though she knew she had no control over my decisions or actions, I knew my habits got under her skin. She'd always say in Spanish, *"Yo no te enseñé eso!"* "I didn't teach you that!" And she was right; she didn't teach me to smoke, drink, or party hard. But I enjoyed that lifestyle because it made me feel free for a while.

One night, I may have gotten a bit too free while hanging out and having a few drinks. I unintentionally shared some details about my relationship with my "friend" that I was trying to hide. My mom's facial expressions and body language made it obvious that she suspected something was happening between this girl and me. She had more than just suspicion and intuition to rely on. First off, she noticed how overly affectionate I was towards this girl, and secondly, I know she overheard certain things in conversations that "friends" don't usually tell each other. I thought about telling my mom about us, but there were numerous reasons not to. I didn't define my relationship with this girl as serious enough to disclose. And experimenting, as I believed I was doing, was not a good enough reason to inform my mom. I also knew Mom would not be jumping for joy if I did tell her.

When the supposed weekend stay expired, my mom took it upon herself to address this and more. I remember being in my mother's bedroom and being asked, *"¿Tú estás con esta tipa?"* "Are you with this chick?" I couldn't lie to her. With a long sigh, a pause, and a deflective response, I said, "Mom, I've been messing with her, and there is nothing wrong with it!" Her reaction was exactly what I thought it would be. She almost sucked up all of the air in the room with the huge gasp she made. In my mother's eyes, there was no such thing as a phase, experiment, or being bisexual. If you engaged in any type of sexual activity with the same sex or were attracted to the same sex, you were gay. Period!

There was shock, disappointment, and judgment on her end, as I had expected. "*Why? ¿Tú sabes de la palabra? ¡Tú sabes que eso a Dios no le agrada!*"

"You know the word! You know the Lord is not pleased with that. Why are you doing this?"

"*Esto le pasa a mujeres que han sido abusadas. ¿Eso a ti no te ha pasado?*"

She told me that women who become lesbians are women who have been abused, and that had never happened to me. My frustration increased not just because I didn't want to hear anything she had to say. It was also the fact that she didn't acknowledge what had happened to me as a child. I didn't like being corrected, but to be misunderstood was a step up. I told her in Spanish,

"*Ay, mami. Por favor. No me juzgues porque tú no estás viviendo bien tampoco!*"

"Oh, Mom, please! Don't judge me because you're not living right either!"

This confession turned into an escalated disagreement I had to leave as an unfinished conversation. I had to walk away. I mean, how far could I have taken it anyway? *Yo no tenía ni adónde caerme muerta!* This is a Spanish saying that depicts how poor you are; when you are so poor, you literally don't even have a place to fall dead on. Meanwhile, this girl was in my ear about her having to leave. She knew what this departure meant for us and kept stressing how she didn't want to leave me and didn't want to drive for six hours alone.

I bought this girl a whole week at the Project Inn. If it were up to my mom, she would have had to take that trip back home right after a bathroom break. I couldn't understand why she kept bringing this up when the agreement was that she would drop me off and go back. She stayed longer than she was supposed to. I knew then that this is where I went wrong, having her drive me to my mom's house.

I have a pretty good memory of many things that have occurred in my life, and I cannot say I remember ever feeling heartbroken about ending what this girl and I had going on. I don't know what clicked in my tiny squirrel brain to AGREE to drive back with her, but it was not a good plan, PERIOD! But, for the sake of storytelling, let's consider some of the most obvious reasons why.

It wasn't a good idea because:

1) I didn't have a penny to my name.
2) I didn't have a solid plan for getting back to Mom's house
3) I had no secure place to stay while I was out there with this girl, not even temporarily.

She didn't even have a secure place to stay.

"*¿Estás hablando en serio?*" "Are you really serious?" my mom asked me in Spanish after I told her what I was about to do next. I tried to reassure my mom I would return because she had all my stuff as collateral. But who was I kidding? I found myself traveling back with this girl without a concrete plan for my return despite all the issues I knew I would encounter beforehand.

We arrived safely at her mother's house, and what I had been telling my mom about her leaving, she was now telling her mom about me. "She'll be leaving in a few days, Mom," she said.

Over those few days, my feelings towards us changed. I had grown so accustomed to receiving the affection, acceptance, and everything I felt I had been longing for that it made me question whether I was willing to give that up. Even though I didn't have deep romantic feelings for her then, a "soul tie" tied us together.

I'll explain what that means in detail in later chapters, but this soul tie kept me connected to her. And so, one thing led to another, and before I knew it, we were seriously considering being together. After she convinced her mother to let me stay at her house until we could get on our feet, we made it official. I will now refer to her as Ava. At nineteen years old, Ava became my second serious relationship and my first same-sex relationship.

Chapter Sixteen

Ava

The beginning of our relationship was like a honeymoon phase. We were inseparable. Anywhere you'd find her, you were bound to find me, and vice versa. Every fun fact became a bonding moment for us. She was like the best friend I never had and the partner I thought I had always wanted. We talked about almost everything—the good, the bad, and the ugly. We would often reminisce about the accomplishments that made us feel like somebody. Those past achievements gave us hope that we could do it all over again and even better with each other. The future we dreamed about would include a home, a loving family, a future that banished instability, a future that paved the way for me to pursue further education, and a career that would make me feel important.

We created this safe space where we dreamt big, and the likelihood of a life without constant struggle seemed within reach. However, this dream quickly crumbled when we were confronted with reality—our reality didn't involve a stable home. It didn't come with the financial resources to match our million-dollar dreams. Our reality felt like being stuck in the deepest valley, far from the mountaintop. Our reality consisted of every fear I dreaded.

We found ourselves living with Ava's mother, who already supported a family of four. With us moving in, we became a struggling family of seven. As you can imagine, space was tight, but so was money. Getting a job seemed like the obvious solution, but job-hunting was much more challenging than anticipated. The worst part about it was that there was nothing I could do to speed up the process; I just had to keep looking, keep waiting for calls, and hope that the right opportunities would come. But waiting seemed to drain the little reservoir of hope I had left.

Desperation forced me to get creative as the needs began to pile up. I had to find ways to substitute the needs, learn to live without it, or find ways to make cash to get what I needed. The only way I knew how to make quick cash was either by dancing or selling items to the pawn shop. I didn't want dancing to be my first choice. So, for a while, we stuck with pawning items that we had. We pawned most of our personal items that had value. This gave us enough cash to grab food, sometimes a pack of cigarettes, and a little gas to stay mobile. But, of course, the money ran out, and so did items to pawn.

This is the part where I had to get creative and make something up to get a free meal from anywhere. When that wasn't an option, I had to steal to eat. If I couldn't do this safely, I just had to settle for whatever small meal was provided that day.

When I struggled with not having enough money to cover the essentials beyond food, I had no choice but to resort to what I didn't want to do. I had to go back to the club. Sometimes, even that wasn't enough, and I had to decide what to buy and go without. Knowing that I had to resort to such extreme measures killed my conscience. I had never gone through anything that had pushed me to this limit, but here I was.

There were clear warning signs that I should've left for many reasons while I still had a chance, but I allowed my heart to take the lead. Jeremiah 17:9 (NIV) gives such a clear depiction of the heart. It goes on to say,

"The heart is deceitful above all things and beyond cure. Who can understand it?"

Your heart will lead you to follow what you want rather than what you need. It can lead you to believe something is right because it feels good, even while going against God's plan for your life. "Follow your heart" is poor advice and can misguide you, especially when you are not measuring your heart against God's truth.

Beyond the attitude of a misled heart, let's consider another reason why I continued to fall into these patterns. I was merely repeating history, falling into a generational cycle. I was mimicking my mother's responses, perpetuating a cycle of codependency, all for the sake of what felt like happiness and love. I was willing to withstand anything and all to have what felt like wholeness. This will sound like I'm going left field, but stay with me. I am going somewhere.

Human beings produce a hormone called Oxytocin. It acts as a neurotransmitter in the brain, becoming responsible for bonding. Hence, the other name for the hormone is "The Bonding Hormone." This hormone is released in men and women but tends to be higher in women. It is also released during labor, and it not only assists in inducing labor and lactation but also assists Mom in bonding with the baby. It is also called the "Love Hormone" because it is present when you fall in love. One of the many interesting facts about Oxytocin is that it is released during sexual activity, which then binds you to the person you are having sex with. This aligns with what the Bible says: "*The two shall become one,*" as mentioned in Genesis 2:24, Mark 19:5, Mark 10:8, and Ephesians 5:31.

I once heard a story about this very thing I am about to share that opened my eyes to the depths of trauma bonding within relationships. They explained how Oxytocin is usually a force for good in the context of motherhood and healthy relationships. But it can quickly become a double-edged sword when forged in toxic relationships. If Oxytocin is the thing that can allow a mother to overlook the excruciating pain that almost physically tore her apart. In that case, imagine how the very same hormone, also reeled through a more binding form of intimacy called "Sex," can also bind people to narcissists with abusive tendencies, which can ultimately tear you apart as well. Let that sink in! This blew me away!

You can't afford to let anyone into your inner circle, let alone choose them as a life partner. Believe that you were created to love and to be loved, and no one should have the right to love you any less on purpose. This explains why my mother tolerated so much when it came to my father and even tolerated so much in marriage with my stepfather. But also why I stayed in so many toxic situations, hoping for the best. My false loyalty to people made me believe I had to stick things out at all costs.

My relationship with Ava had its fair share of dysfunction, but that false loyalty led me to continue using the excuse that no relationship was perfect. Despite all the struggles, sometimes due to our own faults, I still wanted my relationship with Ava. I had redefined what I considered perfect, shaping how I viewed perfection around my lifelong deficiencies. In this altered view, perfection was no longer aligned with what God defined as perfect for me. Rather, it became whatever temporarily satisfied my desires for the moment or a season. It only felt good because I hadn't experienced real goodness.

What have I gotten myself into?

I finally landed an interview for a warehouse and was hired on the spot for a full-time position, just in time for the holidays. The hours were long. Twelve-hour shifts, to be exact, but I was happy to have a job. Without a reliable way to get to work, I still accepted the position. I needed the money and thought, "I'll figure it out."

Ava's mom graciously offered me a ride on my first day. As we arrived at the warehouse, right before I stepped out of the car, her mom turned around and casually asked, "Do you have anything to eat?" I tried to keep a neutral tone, downplaying my need. I knew how jacked up my life was and how dependent I had been on others. I was ashamed of myself and even more ashamed that others knew this, too.

I responded to her question with a nonchalant "No," as if I had been asked if I wanted whipped cream on my latte. She then handed me her Tupperware filled with pasta. Thanks to her, I had something to eat for the day. I made that tiny bowl of pasta last through that long twelve-hour work shift. As soon as the first break hit, I ate enough to keep me going, but not too much, where I wouldn't have anything left.

Unfortunately, that glimmer of hope didn't last too long, as the rug had been pulled out from under me. I had to quit the job because I couldn't get to work. I didn't have a car, and I couldn't scrape up enough gas money to put in Ava's tank until I got my first paycheck. Plus, I hadn't been there long enough to build any relationships with coworkers who might've given me a ride. With the holidays just around the corner, having a secure job painted a picture of how things would've turned out. I was so close to a breakthrough, and I had envisioned the holidays to look like something other than... broke!

At the time, Ava owned a modular home within the development we were living in. However, the house had been vacant for some time, and because of that, the utilities had been disconnected. With one check from this job, we would have restored the house's power and moved in just in time for the holidays. With neither of us having a job, I wondered how long it would be before we could revisit this conversation about having a place of our own. Knowing our situation, Ava's stepfather paid the outstanding balance as a Christmas gift, and we were able to move in just in time for the holidays. Considering that he didn't have much, this was a very kind gesture and what felt like an answered prayer.

We moved our thankful selves into the house dead smack in the middle of December. We were unaware of an issue with the heating system, so the house had no heat. It was so cold that you could see your breath. Our first night there was one of many humbling moments I had experienced. I remember us huddling in the living room, wrapping ourselves with every blanket we owned, using a space heater and the stovetop burners to keep warm. We popped in a DVD and ate a "Poor man's meal"— a bowl of instant rice with canned gravy poured over the top. This was out of my norm since my version of a poor man's meal was more like white rice and a fried egg. That meal felt like a five-star meal. We didn't have much, but I cherished every bit of what we did have. Sadly, this wasn't the last of these types of hard seasons. We kept returning to this struggle, time and time again.

I'll never forget one of the toughest times we went through when we ran out of food entirely. That evening, after realizing we could do nothing, we took a quick ride to her mom's house because she was the only one we could turn to. Her mom had prepared a meal for her family that evening, and when we arrived, one of her siblings was in the middle of their dinner. While Ava went on to speak to her mother about our situation, I gobbled up her sister's leftover pasta that she offered. Normally, I would have hesitated to eat anyone's leftovers, let alone pasta. But at that moment, my hunger trumped all my preferences. Her mom came through as always, but this was another low moment for me.

The struggle eventually made me up the hustle, but the grind was far from easy and over. I didn't own a car or have a driver's license, and there was no public transportation where we lived. There was one taxi cab, one town over, and they charged an arm and a leg to get you from point A to point B. This made it hard to get around conveniently and made it hard to find good opportunities. Even when I did manage to secure a job, my lack of professional experience restricted my opportunities. The opportunities I would get would never bring in the type of income needed for the level of stability I needed and wanted.

You might wonder where Ava was in all of this and what her role was in all of this. Was I the only one grinding? Well, in her defense, her situation was a little different than mine since she had a young child. This complicated her job options and added a few more limitations than mine. However, there was still so much she could have done and didn't do. She just didn't have that "go-getter" quality in her character at the time. I began to realize that she wasn't the person I thought she was, nor the one I thought could help me rebuild my life as we had planned.

I've faced challenges throughout my life that made me a survivor, and our situation unquestionably fell under that category. So, believe me when I say I knew how to survive this. Being aggressive in our approach was the key element in getting through this, and she was passive about survival. To me, passivity and survival didn't even belong in the same sentence.

Ava held a unique perspective on life. As long as the hungry beast hadn't yet entered the field—though there were signs it was approaching—she believed she had time to figure out her next move. It felt like a struggle to keep us both alive while she was the straggler about to get us both killed. But the truth is, you can lead the horse to the water, but you can't make them drink. And that was the situation with Ava and me at that time.

Like my previous relationship, Ava and I had many differences, starting with our cultures. We Puerto Ricans tend to be superstitious by nature. If a baby has hiccups, you stick a piece of thread on their forehead, which would stop the hiccups. If someone has a nosebleed, you place a penny on their forehead, which is supposed to stop the bleeding. Growing up in my household, we had more than just these weird holistic approaches to instant healing. We also had certain *"manias,"* which just means some type of craze about particular things that had to be done in specific manners, and everyone had to follow these *manias*. If you didn't do it like we did, well, then you weren't normal, and we all thought you were weird. Like leaving the paper lid on the mayo, putting your food in the fridge without being covered, or worse, using the kitchen sink for things other than kitchen sink stuff. There were so many things that we consider big no-nos. These things were like automatic *"cocotazos"*– slaps upside the head.

Besides our cultural differences, we had different views on what our social lives should look like, too. She was a social butterfly fueled by people, and I had finally reached that point in my life where I was okay with the small circle of friends I did have. I trusted no one, and my motto was you were guilty until proven innocent. But I especially felt like this about everyone she brought around because we had so many mishaps with so-called "childhood friends" that ended up having other motives. This occurred one too many times. However, I never took a bold stand on this other than being loud. We would make up, and lowkey, I just became bitter, angry, and resentful, and that's where I stayed. So much so that every time I was triggered, those unresolved feelings bubbled up to the surface, and I could not hold back. People were starting to notice.

I had a friend that I had met after moving into town years back. She was one of the older folks in my small circle and played a motherly role in my life. When I was craving a homemade Puerto Rican meal, she was the go-to person to satisfy that craving. But she also gave me a reality check when I needed it. It turns out she knew Ava before I entered the picture, which also meant she knew her ways.

In the beginning stages of my relationship with Ava, we would hang out at who I will refer to as Mama's before we became serious. It was no big secret that Ava was into me and wanted something more than friendship. Mama knew this, too, but she didn't share any excitement about this.

One evening, we were all hanging out in Mama's living room, and she gave me this deep stare that had a language of its own. She broke the silence and translated that stare into this phrase in Spanish: "*Tú te estás metiendo en la boca del león!*" You are putting yourself in the lion's mouth. At first, I didn't fully understand what she meant. However, as the relationship between Ava and me progressed, it became clear that she was right. I was in the lion's mouth. Mama had warned me, but I did not heed the warning.

Turn Back Time

Analyzing all that had happened within the last two years of my life, I wondered how many missed opportunities I had on record in finding my happily ever after. I felt like there were so many unfinished parts of my life, including my past life with Jayce. I had many unanswered questions and did not have the proper closure I felt I deserved. Anger, sadness, and even resentment were still pretty raw. Not to mention that after our relationship ended, I quickly moved on to be with someone else. I never gave myself the time to process, heal, or talk to him about what happened between us.

I still had a way to contact him, so I reached out. After a short conversation, we agreed that a lot needed to be hashed out, and we decided to meet in person. I was already planning a trip to visit my mom, so I took advantage of the trip and decided to meet with him since he was not far from my mom. Ava was not aware of this meeting with Jayce. I was not intentionally trying to be sneaky, but I needed this. I didn't want anything or anyone to stop the closure I was about to receive.

When I arrived at my mom's house, Jayce and I set the time and day to meet. I couldn't believe that this was about to happen. So much had taken place between the last time I saw him till now, and I had no idea what to expect. I wasn't sure how I would feel or if I would have the courage to say what I had rehearsed in my mind. I hoped I would get the proper closure I sought.

On that chilly morning, he pulled up to my mother's house and lightly beeped the horn to signal his arrival. My heart was racing as I approached the car. Getting into the car and seeing his face brought a rush of nostalgia. It felt like yesterday when we were in the same car, hearing the same music he was playing. Even the car scent was still the same. Those emotions hit me like a tidal wave, and our shared history rattled my confidence instantly. For a moment, I found myself overwhelmed by the same feelings that had silenced me in the past.

But I managed to break through that knot in my throat and cut right through the cheap talk. I verbally threw up on him with some rolling of the eyes, flaring of the nostrils, a few outbursts of anger, and some ugly crying. The grand finale was brought on with a few moments of silence and deep, heartfelt apologies. He had his say, and I had mine. And that was it. Did I receive the closure, healing, relief, and clarity I thought I would get by meeting with Jayce? Analyzing this scene now, I knew where he stood in my life, and I got the chance to get things off my chest.

But my heart was still so unsettled. You would think that after I had received what seemed like a heartfelt, genuine apology, it would've been enough for me to close this chapter of my life and move on. Let me clarify that these unsettled feelings were unrelated to how I felt about Jayce romantically. These feelings had nothing to do with him and everything to do with me. Now, hear what I have to say about this because this is now a thirty-four-year-old, healed, whole me, analyzing nineteen-year-old broken, lost me.

The unsettled feelings were still present after I got what I thought I needed and wanted because the apology wasn't enough. Why? Because there were deeper issues at play beyond the heartbreak. It dawned on me that I had never confronted anything or anyone who had hurt me, and I had never really healed from ... anything in my life. I just always kept pushing. I pushed beyond the pain. I moved beyond the disappointment. I kept going no matter what.

I viewed my ability to keep moving as a strength. But moving on without ever acknowledging what had been broken or wounded and never taking the time to heal did damage—not just to myself but to others as well.

I mistakenly identified moving on with anthems like "Healed," "Strong," "Invisible," or "Ms. Independent." I had this mindset that if I kept telling myself I wasn't angry, hurt, or sad, the feelings didn't exist. This mindset caused me to bypass every opportunity to reflect, recover, and heal.

When going through things, I had to get good at burying feelings; otherwise, it would hinder what I believed was progress. But concealing those unhealed parts didn't fail in preventing the symptoms of that unresolved pain. Which then manifested into patterns of unhealthy entanglements. Leaving me more wounded than I was in the first place. I was so unprepared to handle life's complexities. I sure didn't have a clue on how I was supposed to shield myself from life's inevitable disappointments or people's inconsistencies. Let alone learning how to identify and regulate my own inconsistencies. Forgiveness could have cured so many of these wounds. Yet forgiveness wasn't even a concept that I knew how to apply to others or even myself.

While I never acknowledged those unsettling feelings towards Jayce and so many others in my life as unforgiveness, they were under the category of unforgiveness. My lack of acknowledgment didn't place a pause button on what unforgiveness was doing to me. We often form these ideas about the conditions that must be met before releasing those who wronged us. We might tell ourselves, "I'll forgive them if they apologize to me," or "I'll let go of my grudge if I get a chance to speak my mind." And then there's the classic, "They don't deserve forgiveness!" I've had these same feelings towards many people in my life. Even after receiving apologies of all sorts, it still didn't resolve anything in me.

As many of us have heard, unforgiveness is like a cancer. Once it enters one part of the body, it can run rampant, causing your body to deteriorate entirely and quickly. I was deteriorating as I kept replaying that bitter, painful melody that opened up what we call a "soul wound."

Eventually, my unresolved pain quickly went from unforgiveness to also wanting vengeance. I would find satisfaction in wishing that life would catch up to the ones who hurt me, making them pay for what they did. Convincing myself that if I got the revenge I wanted, I could let go of what they had done to me because they had paid the price for what they did to me. But I've discovered that even when justice is served, and they get what they deserve, the punishment doesn't always bring the peace or closure you think you'll receive.

So, how did I manage to let the offenders go? Well, after so many years and so much wasted time, I had to realize that I survived. I had to accept that I couldn't change what happened, and I began viewing the experiences as life lessons rather than life sentences.

I had to let God heal my heart, and I had to stop trying to heal my own heart with my wounded hands. Have you ever seen a surgeon handle a heart with wounded hands? Never! Or have you ever seen a heart surgeon perform their own heart surgery? Never! But I kept resisting God's care about the matters of my heart and soul because I felt like I could heal myself. And that kept me in that cycle of unforgiveness, causing me to bleed on people who didn't even inflict the wounds. I paid a hefty price for that choice.

I had spent so much of my precious, valuable time and energy placing blame and pointing fingers at those whom I held responsible for my pain. Whether or not they acknowledged it, these people I was angry with weren't losing sleep because of how I felt. They were carrying on with their lives. MY HEALING WAS NOT THEIR RESPONSIBILITY; IT WAS MINE!

I had to learn that people's decisions always catch up to them. I didn't have to tell the world what they had done to me. I didn't have to warn others about them. If you plant bad seeds, you'll reap bad fruit. An example of this is found in the book of Samuel, which tells the story of David and King Saul. King Saul made David's life hell for years because of his insecurities and envy. King Saul had been pursuing him relentlessly, and David did not retaliate. Not because he wasn't able to. Because, remember, David was a man of war. He didn't retaliate because he honored King Saul as God's anointed and feared the Lord. David had the opportunity to take King Saul out when he went into the cave and cut off a piece of King Saul's robe. But he didn't.

Instead, he said this:

"This day, you have seen with your own eyes how the Lord delivered you into my hands in the cave. Some urged me to kill you, but I spared you; I said, "I will not lay my hand on my lord because he is the Lord's anointed." See, my father, look at this piece of your robe in my hand! I cut off the corner of your robe but did not kill you. See that there is nothing in my hand to indicate that I am guilty of wrongdoing or rebellion. I have not wronged you, but you are hunting me down to take my life. May the Lord judge between you and

me. And may the Lord avenge the wrongs you have done to me, but my hand will not touch you." See 1 Samuel 24:10-12 (NIV)

Mighty God! That is honor! In the later chapters, specifically chapter 31, we find that King Saul falls on his own sword after a fierce battle with an enemy of the nation of Israel. He took himself out! David didn't have to do a thing. Not that we should celebrate when life catches up to those who want to be our enemies, as David also didn't celebrate his death. But the point I'm making is that people who do you wrong intentionally... their choices catch up without your help.

James 2:13 (NIV) says, *"Mercy triumphs over judgment."* That means God always wants to extend mercy. This explains His patient nature with humankind, even though we continuously defy Him. But that's a different topic for a different day. As God has demonstrated forgiveness, mercy, and grace towards me, even when I deserve judgment, I can do the same for others.

I have also learned that God will forgive those who truly repent. Even the ones I have believed to deserve nothing but judgment because of their actions. But people can change! People can grow up, and we just have to get over it! We can't be walking around here like little angry Jonahs? Mad at God because He didn't pour His wrath on people who caused us pain? Who are we to hold the sin against them if God has dropped the charges? A small disclaimer— I'm not referring to crimes that deserve time. Because God is merciful, but sometimes you aren't saved from the consequences. But back to what I was saying—learn to forgive easily, and if the offenders don't repent, let God deal with that, too. Again, healing is our responsibility; vengeance is His. See Romans 12:19.

At the end of the day, forgiveness is a choice you are making for yourself, not for the offender. You forgive so that you can be released from the offense. This gives God permission to heal you and to work on your behalf. It also does not allow the enemy to have a foothold in your life.

The antidote for unforgiveness is... LETTING GO AND LETTING GOD! You bless them and release them as often as needed to ensure your heart stays pure and doesn't get contaminated with that poison. In the later chapters, I'll share my experiences of forgiving others and the results of walking in true forgiveness.

But going back to the story of my closure with Jayce, I returned home not understanding why I felt the way I did. I didn't trust anyone enough to speak openly about what happened. I just had my notebook and pen, writing down what I thought would remain unspoken.

Chapter Seventeen

Turbulence

Ava and I decided to sell the modular home we were living in. A few weeks later, we moved into what we considered an instant upgrade. We were so caught up in wanting a finished product that we were ready to give up what we had, believing it was worth the trade. Someone say, "message!" The apartment we moved into was within a newly built development, specifically for college students who needed a cheaper alternative to live near campus. This would explain why there were so many amenities that we were going bananas for. It was a fully furnished apartment with all brand-new furniture and appliances. It had brand-new beds, a TV, washer and dryer, phone, cable, and internet service. They even provided an allotted credit that would be put towards the monthly electric bill. Moved by another new beginning, I swept our issues under the rug. Including these feelings, I had about our relationship that had nothing to do with the obvious problems.

With the payment she received for selling the house, she paid the rent six months in advance. This eliminated much of the stress attached to our major financial issues. It should have marked the perfect opportunity for us to rebuild our foundation as I had always imagined it. Yet, I could not shake off this lingering feeling of dissatisfaction.

I believe this was the period of my life when the concept of God began to re-emerge slowly. It was a time when my logic and emotions no longer seemed to align with what I had committed to. Everything that had made me consider leaving her had been resolved. We had the upgraded apartment that we both wanted. We had the cushion in the bank. We had jobs. We had everything I had fought her to have, and now I wasn't happy. So, what was the problem?

I was becoming uncomfortable with the idea of us being a couple. But I didn't want to believe that this was the real problem underneath it all. Attempting to find relief from what was tormenting me, I reached out to people I knew who had come from similar backgrounds, hoping to hear that this was a normal process that everyone went through and that I was good.

A friend shared with me that she also used to feel guilty about her lifestyle. But as she continued to live out her choices, she just stopped feeling like it was wrong. Hearing this from someone who had been in this lifestyle longer than I had brought clarity. It pushed me towards the belief that the discontentment within the relationship was a result of the indoctrination instilled through teachings of the religion that had systematically convinced me that my lifestyle was wrong. This deception settled the matter for a while until that sinking feeling returned.

I have this memory of when that light bulb really went off in my head. Ava and I were at a store grabbing a few things to decorate our new home. I remember specifically being in the aisle where all the bathroom decor was, and I began looking through the different themes, designs, towels, rugs, etc. While looking, I saw that she picked something off the shelf, and I gave her that stank look and said, "I don't like that," expecting her to put it back because I didn't like it! She gave me that side look and said, "Carmen, I live there too. I want to decorate MY house, too!"

I wasn't shocked by her response, but her response made me realize how I was silently defending my position, forgetting that Ava was also a woman. Not that there's a gender role assigned to home decor, but the fact that I wasn't sure where I fit in felt awkward. We weren't following the traditional couple dynamics, and things were different, whether I wanted to admit it or not. This wasn't just because it was my first same-sex relationship; it felt out of order because I was navigating a connection with another person who was built and wired just like me. It felt like I was competing with another woman for a role that was already supposed to be mine.

More of these "out of order" feelings surfaced as we tried to build a nuclear family unit. It felt strange when I tried to define my role in her child's life or figure out what I needed to be for her child. In a typical, "healthy" nuclear family, you usually have a clear idea of who assumes which role—Not just in terms of domestic tasks, because let's face it, some men are better cooks or clean better than most women. I'm going a little deeper than that. I am talking about the spiritually assigned roles of a husband/ wife and mother/father.

Biblically, the man/father plays the role of protector and leader within the family, bringing a sense of safety and divine order. This reflects the image of the heavenly father through leadership, authority, and vision. The man is seen as the priest of the home, with responsibilities that extend beyond the physical realm.

Most children who grow up without paternal guidance develop identity issues. I am not saying that single moms can't raise children well, but mothers can't give what fathers are built to provide. Raising respectful, brilliant, and civil men and women without an active father complicates things much more than they should. While single moms have been killing it, I'm sure they would have preferred the father to be present.

On the other hand, the woman's role is often viewed as setting the temperature within the home and offering comfort and tender care. She also holds authority; she is a helper, a mate, and a nurturer. A woman's presence or absence can also significantly impact a child's upbringing, just like the absence of a father or male figure can. Although I was also built to embody these roles, Ava was the original nurturer, and I was the manufactured one.

My role never felt entirely natural to me, despite my efforts to normalize it. I just didn't have the language to articulate what I was feeling. While I wanted to believe in the idea that love transcends gender and that happiness is what matters the most, I couldn't shake what was happening inside me. I was trying so hard to ignore this conviction. At the time, I wasn't even familiar with the term "conviction." I had distanced myself from anyone who could've preached to me. I didn't attend church and cut off all access to preachers or a Bible. So, God was dealing with me in a very unorthodox manner. But I couldn't see that through this thing called conviction, God was giving me the opportunity to repent. Someone say, grace and mercy.

"It is His kindness that leads us into repentance." Romans 2:4

Honestly, I didn't want God to be the reason I had to leave this relationship. I would have preferred to walk away for other reasons. I knew that if I walked away because of Jesus, I would be hated for it, mocked, judged, and misunderstood. Sometimes, God wants us to cut ties with something or someone, and we hang on because of comfort. We hang on because we fear all the backlash that will come with letting go. We think we are staying for all the right reasons, and really, we hang on for all the wrong reasons. And God, being the gentleman that He is, doesn't force us to do anything. Just like He didn't force me to do anything but gave me what I wanted and allowed me to have things my way. We make way for the hammer to come down out of our disobedience. And in my case, the hammer was pretty heavy and painful, to say the least.

Remember when I said I wanted to walk away for reasons other than Jesus? How I wish I hadn't been so rebellious and stubborn. I could've saved myself from so much trouble. Not long after I ignored that conviction, Ava and I hit another rough patch. Cue the dramatic music, please! TAN TAN TAN. Ava discovered a secret I thought I would take to my grave.

My mom always told me to keep my secrets in my head and never write them down. Even as a kid, I always got busted about secret things because I journaled everything. She called me Doug Funny. Only 90's kids know what I'm talking about. But anyway, Ava found the notebook, y'all! THE NOTEBOOK! The one where I jotted down my experience with Jayce.

Ava's reaction was nothing short of intense. I had never seen her act like this. I didn't know what to say in my defense. All I could say was a string of apologies, insisting that nothing happened between Jayce and me and explaining why I met with him. The truth was true, but proving it when only two people were present made it tough. She never trusted me the same way after that. The constant questioning and the assumption that I was the worst became the new norm. The benefit of the doubt? Well, that was off the table.

We pressed forward, but the relationship took a darker turn, filled with more toxicity, anger, and verbal clashes—mostly initiated by me. Things we never imagined were now part of our everyday lives, like constant disrespect and physical confrontations. Along with the relationship drama, our money was funny. We couldn't cover the bills, and before we knew it, we were getting the boot for not paying rent. We returned to her mom's place, and all three of us squeezed into one room with our belongings. Another holiday season broke, with no apartment and no money. That's when we found ourselves back on the grind, doing what we needed to do to survive. I got caught up with some pretty sketchy stuff and people, not realizing the risks I was taking with my freedom and, honestly, with my very life. It had to be God's mercy and grace that kept me because there was no other explanation. And I probably will not know the backstory of how I made it out safe and alive in some of these situations I got involved in until I have that face-to-face conversation with God.

The Exit

I pulled some strings, and Ava and I secured an apartment in February of that following year after we lost the last apartment. We got that apartment by the skin of our teeth. Ava managed to lose most of our first month's rent and security deposit the night before it was due—talk about anxiety! Once again, her mom swooped in to save the day, giving us the remainder of the money we needed to sign the lease. Our total payout was $900. I remember signing the lease with $899 in cash, and we paid the last dollar in four quarters. Yeah, that's how much of an "almost moment" this was. A true story! As embarrassing as it was paying that last dollar in quarters, I didn't care. I had a home. Even if I had to pay with a gazillion pennies in socks to get that apartment, I would've done it in a heartbeat.

We made the dumb move of getting rid of the furniture Ava had when we moved into that furnished apartment. So, all we had were the basics—a mattress, dishes, pots, blankets, and a few pieces of furniture. Nothing fancy, but it was home—my home—a home I intended to keep no matter what it took. With that mindset, I established some terms and conditions for our relationship to safeguard my peace, sanity, and security.

Things seemed to be going well between us, and as time passed, the good times made it easy to fully embrace what I believed was my happiness—regardless of whether it was accepted by others or even by God Himself. I reconsidered my feelings and concerns about being part of a blended family, my role in it, procreation, and even the possibility of marriage with her if it came across the table. I was just going with the flow because everything was going well.

Again, we found ourselves in the same mess and eventually called it quits. We finally broke up. We weren't claiming each other as a couple, but our actions said another thing. In reality, all the breakup did was move her from one room to another within the same place. But the breakup also made her free to do whatever she wanted to do. She was single and didn't have to keep our breakup a secret. Of course, the same applied to me, too.

I tried to embrace my single status by seeking comfort from others who seemed interested in making me the object of their affection. However, her singleness brought on more than I could emotionally handle. It felt as if the breakup had somehow favored her because of how much it seemed like she was gaining through her new liberty. As I had shared, I harbored resentment towards Ava because I held her responsible for much of the loss I had experienced. I hated that I seemed to care more about our well-being than she did, and I hated the responsibility of caring for a family when all I wanted was someone to take care of me. I acknowledge that I chose to stay and stick it out, whether it was an educated decision or not. Still, the repercussions of this decision fueled my growing animosity towards her.

I no longer had many moments of kindness, gentleness, compassion, or grace toward her. I just resented her more than I ever had. Given our shared history and living situation, those once clear-cut boundaries became somewhat blurry, landing our relationship status in the "it's complicated" zone. Cutting ties wasn't as straightforward because of how intertwined our lives were. To distract myself from my messy life, I worked tirelessly. The motivation to work so much also stemmed from the need to secure my apartment. This added another layer to my already deepening depression because I had no life outside of demands.

I was on a difficult, demanding schedule, working ten or more consecutive days with shifts ranging from twelve to sixteen hours a day. My workday kicked off as early as 5 am and wrapped up as late as 10:30 pm. On the days I had to walk to work, it would add 2 ½ hours to my day on top of my work schedule. It was an hour and fifteen-minute walk to get there and another hour and fifteen-minute walk to get home. The emotional toll was already overwhelming, but now I was physically drained. The stress piled up to the point where sleep became hard to catch. I resorted to sleeping pills, sex, alcohol, weed, and cigarettes. These were the coping mechanisms I used to find peace. But the relief I had found in these temporary fixes was short-lived, pushing me to seek these quick fixes more often.

It Went Too Far

Ava was making her way to the apartment, and things had escalated from the ongoing arguments of the day. We had become so toxic that we never knew how far it would go. Long story short, she walked into the apartment fueled, and I was already on edge. The insults kept going back and forth, and the aggression picked up so much that I had to ask her to leave. She refused, no matter what I said. I even threatened to call the cops if she didn't leave because, at that point, nothing would make her budge. I didn't care for a healthy ending. I didn't care if her leaving that night meant she would be cut out of my life forever. I just wanted her gone.

She finally agreed to leave peacefully, but not without one final move to push me over the edge. Before exiting, she entered the bedroom and sat on the floor next to a lamp I had near the door. I lay on my bed, physically drained, and she then asked, "Carmen, can I make a call from your phone?" I handed over the phone, believing she would do as she said. I then heard her talking with someone over the phone, which she had been talking to at the time. I didn't care to confirm whether she was pretending to be speaking to that person or she was actually making that call. But that surge of anger and mania returned. I charged at her with everything I had, and in the middle of this, the lamp in the room toppled over, putting us into total darkness. We found ourselves on the floor, but nothing was visible; I couldn't even see my hand in front of me. Once we had regained our composure and realized how far our toxicity had gone, we knew that this had to be the end.

We eventually were able to make amends but not to restore the relationship. Even though the relationship was over, I felt like I still owed myself a fair shot at doing life without Ava and without the need to leave the town. I finally took the plunge and signed up for cosmetology school—something I'd been itching to do for years. At the same time, I hustled to find a job that paid better. I got an interview, and it looked like it went well. So, from then on, I just had to wait for them to contact me with their decision.

A few days after this interview, I remember sitting on my back porch on a hot summer evening. I had a moment of reflection, which led me into a heartfelt, genuine conversation with God. Although I didn't want to have a deep relationship with Him, I did acknowledge His existence. I knew that this was the last straw for me. I promised Him that if I didn't get that job, I'd pack up and head home with no ands, ifs, or buts.

Oh! How often do we overlook that He is God Almighty? We forget that His ways are not our ways, and His thoughts are higher than ours. He sees from the end to the beginning and the beginning to the end. While I knew of God, I didn't truly understand His ways. I had been filtering Him through the lens of my own human understanding. I didn't even realize that having this genuine conversation with the Lord was really me giving Him permission to work. Proverbs 16:9 (ESV) beautifully captures this truth:

"The heart of man plans his way, but the LORD establishes his steps."

It reminds us that while we may make our plans, God ultimately directs our steps, leading us on a path we may not have imagined for ourselves.

I finally received a response from the job I had applied for. It was a postcard stating that my background check and drug test came back clear, along with the date and time for orientation, just as they had promised. I felt like I could stop holding my breath now. But remember Proverbs 16:9 as I tell you the next part of this story.

Orientation day had arrived, and I could feel the excitement bubbling up within me. It was the beginning of the comeback I had dreamt of—a job paying me twice as much, where I could support myself while going to school. It was the moment I had been waiting for. I pulled up to the facility and made it through the main entrance. I pressed the buzzer, eagerly waiting to tell them why I was there. "You said your name was Carmen?" the woman asked. "Yes," I replied. I sensed the confusion in her tone as she asked me to hold for a moment, and my chest began to tighten as I anxiously waited for her response. I could detect disappointment from a mile away, and this sounded a lot like disappointment.

"Carmen, it appears that we made multiple attempts to extend the offer via phone and email, and we did not receive a response. Unfortunately, we could not reach you, and the position has been filled. Currently, we have no available positions." The woman from HR said. I was speechless. I didn't know what to say but refused to let this slide. Determined to prove them wrong, I went home to research and pull out all the receipts. I needed this job! I thoroughly checked all voicemails, emails, and spam to ensure I hadn't missed anything. I didn't find any communication besides what I had received in the mail.

Having gained more experience in hiring processes since then, almost always, there is a call and/or email that will follow confirming the offer. But even at that, it didn't make sense that I didn't get a call when all of my lines of communication had been kept open, and I wasn't able to find an email with the offer. I didn't know how to move on from here. There was no plan B. All my options had been exhausted, and there were no more quick fixes; time had run its course.

After processing everything that had happened, it dawned on me that what happened was no mistake. God's divine intervention orchestrated this. If I didn't want to believe this was God's doing, Oh ord, I don't know what it would have taken for me to get it. God had listened to me loud and clear that day when I had that heart-to-heart with Him on my back porch. He heard surrender, not that cheap bargain I tried to make with Him.

Soon after, I arranged to give up the apartment and return home with Mom. And if I still didn't believe this was a God thing and I needed more confirmation, check this out! I didn't even have to pay for the ticket to return home. Someone paid for my train ticket. It cost me absolutely nothing to leave, although it cost me everything to stay! And just like that, I hopped on the train and left everything I knew behind.

Being in a different place gave me the time and mental space to really process and work through everything that had gone down. I reflected on the breakups, the instability, the stress, the ups and downs, and all the losses, especially the most recent thing that happened in my relationship with Ava. No matter how hard I tried, memories of her just triggered me. Memories were triggered by simple things like songs that played on the block. Anyone who came around that reminded me of her caused that grief and pain to resurge. Thankfully, there were a couple of hundred miles in the distance between us. If not, I would've tried to find her, attempting to ease the grief. The physical distance kept us apart. Time, however, was still within my control, and I made the time to speak with her daily.

Since we were both in unstable situations when we broke up, I was concerned about her well-being. But we also had this toxic codependency thing going on. No matter how destructive we were together or how bad we were for each other, we felt this sense of responsibility for one another. It was almost like we forgot that there was a reason why we were not together anymore.

This is a perfect example of that "soul tie" I said I would take the time to explain. A soul tie is what knits you at the soul, binding you to another through a form of intimacy. Different types of soul ties come on through various forms of intimacy, such as the one between David and Jonathan. They were knitted at the soul through friendship, a different form of intimacy that did not involve sex. But sex, on the other hand, had become the gateway that banded me to Ava, not allowing me to leave even though

I wanted to leave. This could have easily been broken through renouncing, repentance, and deliverance. But these were things I didn't know existed.

Chapter Eighteen

Pride Comes Before The Fall

I had grown so accustomed to always having someone available to run to when I needed comfort that being *this* single felt strange. Choosing to handle my junk without using someone to soften the blow was hard. But the good thing is that moving back home gave me a sense of community, and having this helped with the sudden changes. I began connecting with all my cousins again. Yes! These are the same daredevils I mentioned at the beginning of my story. One of those cousins lived right across from my mother's apartment building, and the others lived in the apartment buildings down the street. I spent summer nights hanging out with them, and we spent a lot of time laughing and reminiscing about our *fuego-fire* Pentecostal days.

Reflecting on those moments, I see how our laughter about sister so-and-so catching the Holy Ghost masked a deep longing to go back to a time when things were different and simple. The jokes always led us into deep conversations about our personal Jesus stories. At the end of the night, we found ourselves watching powerful testimonies on YouTube of individuals who had gone through crazy transformations through their encounters with Jesus. And it was a complete type of freedom. Not the "I'm kind of free" and I'm struggling but a resounding "I'm totally free!"

After watching these videos, I couldn't help but wonder about my own life—both the present and the afterlife. I was worried that living out this YOLO (You Only Live Once) lifestyle might come at the expense of one day discovering that eternity without God was a real thing. I was afraid that I would find out that God was not a fear tactic used by religion to control you. When I was alone with my thoughts, I thought of all those people who were transformed by God's power and thought, "Could this power be real enough to transform my life too?"

I have an uncle who attended a church that hosted youth services every Friday night. Like clockwork, he'd text me, inviting me to join. I was still a bit skeptical about attending an actual church because the last time I stepped into a church, I was hoping to find God, and instead, I left with the same heavy baggage I came in with. Nonetheless, I gave his church a shot. As I walked into the sanctuary, I saw a bunch of young folks going all out in worship—hands in the air, completely lost in the moment. And man, it had me thinking. Could I really find more fulfillment in Jesus than the temporary satisfaction I had found in the world?

Watching those young kids worship felt like it was possible, and watching them made me want to join them in worship and raise my hands, too. So, there I'd be, eyes closed, head bowed, whispering, "I want God like that too." The guilt of my sins stung in God's presence. And that should've been the moment that I surrendered my life to God. But I wasn't ready. What stopped me was the love of this world and the love for my sin. I knew that if I decided to have a relationship with God, I would have to end my relationship with the world. And I wasn't ready for that.

Although I understood that the pleasures of this world wouldn't last, I was hesitant to dive deep into a relationship with God because I associated church with deprivation. I liked my party life. I loved to drink and get high. I loved the club scene. And I wanted no part in the portion of this walk that included the death of self. But I also didn't believe that God could transform my life in a way that would kill the cravings for the things that weren't good for me. It never occurred to me that the kind of "dying to self " God required would be the very thing that would lead me to know Him in a way that would bring lasting fulfillment.

As I mingled with new faces, I stumbled upon fresh distractions as a young single woman. These diversions overshadowed my commitment to meeting with Jesus on those Friday nights. Work and clubbing became the main chapters of my life during this stretch, and things appeared to be going well for me. But only for a season. Yes, look at your neighbor and say, "But only for a season!"

"There is a way that appears to be right, but in the end, it leads to death." Proverbs 14:12 (NIV)

I landed a job, enrolled in school, and held the keys to my first apartment—alone! Life was falling into place, and I was proud of my accomplishments. Immature me wanted everyone who doubted me, especially people like Ava, to see that I had moved way beyond where they thought they had left me. I invited her to visit with all expenses paid. She agreed, and everything unfolded as I thought it would. One week of spontaneity undid any clarity and healing that might've happened during the four months of separation. Inviting her back in drew me back into a vulnerable state, causing me to fall back into the place I was supposed to distance myself from. I re-opened wounds.

After her departure, the ache of loneliness surged again. Worse than I had felt before. Loneliness greeted me late at night. Unable to deal with the loneliness, I gave in to what I saw as opportunities to cure the loneliness. But they were very unhealthy, toxic ways of "moving on." More soul ties, I should say. I got tangled up with people who seemed to care about me, and I fell for it every time. I settled for whatever little bit of themselves they offered.

My Godfather came into my life during this period. Again, this was God's love and mercy swinging by. I hadn't seen my Godfather since I was a child. I saw him at a church I had visited when I moved back in with Mom. He gave me his contact information, and we stayed in touch.

I remember the day I got my apartment; he swung by to bring me a few household items. Along with this, he bought me this navy-blue leather NIV Bible. I didn't see this book as a gift. Regardless, I said thank you, took the Bible, and stored it in my closet. One night, while I was getting ready for bed, I had a sudden urge to get that blue leather Bible out of the closet. I opened up this brand-new Bible, not knowing what I was looking for. But that one night turned into a few nights, and before I knew it, I was reading small portions of scripture every night before bed, even when I didn't fully understand all that I was reading. Then, something happened—I began to see how the Bible addressed so many of the things I loved as things that grieved God's heart. I then realized how broken I really was and how much I needed God.

Although I grew up in church and had experiences with the Lord, I had never really read the Bible in depth on my own. It wasn't something I'd ever taken the time to do, nor was it enforced. I just knew whatever they taught at the kid's Bible study. Considering all the churchy, religious experiences I had gone through, I expected nothing but judgment from God at this point, mainly because of how I had been living. But as I started reading the scripture, I felt the opposite. Reading the word wasn't bringing fear. If anything, it compelled me to reassess my life through the lens of God's word. Hebrews 4:12 (NIV) says:

"For the word of God is living and active, sharper than any two-edged sword, piercing to the division of soul and of spirit, of joints and of marrow, and discerning the thoughts and intentions of the heart."

Hebrews 4:12 was happening to me in the privacy of my own home. The word of God was becoming real and cutting me to the core. It was changing me, and I didn't even know it. But satan wasn't about to let it be that easy for me to break free. He had to devise another plot that he knew I would fall for. Again, he used nothing new and used my weaknesses against me because he does not play fair, but can someone say, "But God!"

The Painful Exchange

I started a music project with a few local artists when Ava and I lived together. When I left, the project was left unfinished. The artists reached out, asking me to return and complete the track in the studio. While I wanted to go, the dilemma was that this would take me back to where Ava and I once lived together, doing more damage than good. God had been working on my heart during this time, and returning to record the hook could have led me in a different direction if things had gone as expected. Regardless, I went away against all the facts and possibilities of emotional and spiritual setbacks. I just felt like this could've been "My big break." That felt like a good enough reason to downplay the potential damage. It was just a weekend trip, right? What harm could come from a two-day trip?

I got Ava to pick me up at the train station on a Friday afternoon. We had not seen each other for about two months since her last visit. Here I was with her, driving down from my pick-up destination, doing things we used to do, just like the old times. I was living in the moment, not realizing how this would affect me later on. After arriving at Ava's place, I was picked up and headed straight to the studio. I celebrated the completion and success of the track by having some drinks during and after the session. By the time I returned to her place, I was pretty intoxicated, and unfortunately, this led to some regrettable choices that set me back emotionally.

Sunday was the day I was scheduled to leave. Yet, the familiarity began to resist the plan. I postponed the trip and rescheduled it for a few days later, thinking I just needed a few more days to get it together or "get it out of my system." With each passing day, it was becoming harder and harder to leave. So, what happened between that Friday and then? Where were all these feelings coming from? I began to reconsider us. Completely forgetting our history and wanting to give us another try.

If I had severed ties with her, I would have kept everything I had—my stability, independence, and much more. However, if I chose to re-enter the relationship (which she offered as an option), I risked forfeiting all that I had worked so hard to obtain, all in the name of what I considered to be love. This would also involve sacrificing the small spark that had ignited between God and me.

What kept me so drawn to her is that no matter what we went through, no matter what she had put me through, what I had put her through, I didn't have to fight to be accepted. I didn't have to jump through hoops to get her attention or impress her. And to think I could be giving this up again, not knowing if this would ever come knocking at my door? That felt like a huge loss. But another thing that made me reconsider—I was scared to lose my family. Ava's family became my own in every sense. I spent holidays and birthdays with them. We celebrated each other's milestones and accomplishments. They had been there through it all. I had my own family, but there was a disconnect, and the bond I shared with Ava's family was something I lacked with my own.

On Sunday, April 24, 2010, on my 22nd birthday, one week after I arrived at her place, I found myself silently sitting on her mother's back porch with my thoughts. I was hours away from my scheduled departure. As much as I knew this was my last opportunity to walk away entirely, it was also her last time asking me what I wanted. I heard the seriousness and emotion in her voice, ready to accept whatever the response was. "Do you want to be with me or not?" As I breathed deeply with tears streaming down my face, I responded, "I want to, and I want to be with you, but I can't!" I could tell that she was confused and heartbroken about my response. "What does that mean, Carmen?" She asked. "You can't, and you won't understand!" I said. What was it that wouldn't allow me to say yes to her? Was this fierce defiance coming from the fear of reliving the trauma that we experienced in the past? Or was it coming from something else?

We both sensed the tension building, each experiencing it differently. Ava placed pressure on me to decide for us, and I knew that I had to make a choice. Inevitably, my yes or no would come at a cost. I knew that these little visitation rights Ava and I had, this thing we had going on, had to end. I knew this had to be goodbye, not for a little while. It had to be for good or else. I can't really explain what that "or else" meant. If I didn't cut ties that day, I would lose more than what I perceived as a loss.

Every time I was close to saying yes to her, this siren went off in my spirit, "It is time to walk away!" For the first time, I willingly accepted that I couldn't be with her. I could no longer ignore it. I had fully acknowledged and accepted that this was coming from God. This was once again another divine intervention. I know that God wanted to deliver me from so much more than this lifestyle I was trying to keep at bay. But it had to start with this first. I was sure that this was a God thing because, despite my best efforts, nothing within my strength could sever the ties I had with her. I now know, by information, that my Bible-thumping, holy-roller, Christian Godfather had been interceding on my behalf. He had been toiling this hard ground in the spirit ever since he reconnected with me. He was sowing seeds of love and truth even when I didn't like it. Even when I didn't want it. As James 5:16 (NIV) says, "*It is the prayer of a righteous man that availed much.*"

During that eight-hour train ride, doubt clouded my thoughts. I questioned if I had made a mistake—was my "yes" to God driven by the fear of eternity without Him? Would this decision give me an unfulfilled life? As thoughts and emotions consumed me, I just remember crying for a long time. I knew that this would be the last time I would see her. My sadness quickly turned into anger towards God as I began to shake my fist at Him. I began charging Him for everything that went wrong in my life, including His recent request to leave Ava, which felt much more like a command.

Yes, I knew that He was a sovereign God, but I did not like His sovereignty at that moment. If He was an all-knowing God, wasn't He aware of everything I have been through? All the things that I had lost over the years. Certainly, He could not be asking me to lay this down, too. I wanted His sovereignty to cater to my preferences and my desires. Why could He not change His mind on how He viewed my sin? I would've been willing to leave everything else. But this? This was hard!

I had hoped that the truth about my so-called sinful life was lost somewhere in translation and that maybe this one part wasn't as literal as I had believed. I had only wished that God would approve of me returning back. All I could focus on was what I had to nail on the cross and not on who had been nailed on the cross for me and my sins. Why couldn't there be an exception for this one thing? I wasn't harming anyone; I wasn't stealing or taking lives. Where was the real danger in my actions? I hated this narrow path.

Yet, I never realized that although I was not committing the worst of things in my own eyes, I was inflicting pain on God every time I turned away from His gift of salvation in favor of my sinful ways. Having just faced one of the most challenging decisions of my life, I longed for Jesus to meet me halfway. Jesus did meet halfway, just not in the way I had envisioned.

Chapter Nineteen

The Meeting With Jesus

My father agreed to pick me up from the train station and take me back to my apartment. Getting into the car there was a very civil greeting—a simple hello and no "Happy Birthday." When I reminded him of what day it was, he then said happy birthday, but it lacked emotion and enthusiasm. Maybe he was going through his own stuff. Who knows? But it added fuel to the fire. I would've found so much comfort in sharing what was in my heart with someone at this time. But opening up to him, or anyone for that matter, would've only added more ammo to the negative thoughts about me and this relationship. There was no empathy for me in this. If anything, it was better that it happened this way.

The dread was coming on heavier as we got closer to my apartment. As I walked up the steps to my door, I took a deep breath, unlocked the door, laid all my stuff down, and sat at the kitchen table. There was a moment of silence where it felt like time stood still, and then... I broke down. I began to weep inconsolably. None of my usual go-to comforts felt like they could offer me the relief they once did. Not a stiff drink, not sex, not a smoke, not a party. Nothing!

To add to this, it was my birthday. It was a day that was supposed to be filled with celebration, laughter, and joy, a day that was supposed to feel like a new beginning. And nothing about this day felt anything close to that. But it was right here, in this exact moment, where I believe I came to the end of myself.

I finally cried out to God from the depths of my soul, the only way I knew how. The words that came out of my mouth were not elegant. This prayer wasn't high and lofty. The words were not filled with poetic shenanigans that I believed would impress God enough to grab His attention. This cry was deep, messy, desperate, and loud. There were even a few words I mouthed with no sound.

"Lord, if this is not what you want for me, I am okay with that! But I need you to be the one to get me out because I can't!"

This was my prayer. This was "surrender." At that moment, I felt alone. But I know now that God was holding my hand through this whole thing. When that prayer of surrender was released, I imagine He began the wedding preparations for me as His bride. Yes, there was a lot of work to do, as there is much preparation to prepare any bride. But without hesitation, He leaned back, cracked His knuckles, and pulled out the blueprints stored in my book of destiny.

Jesus, the foreman of my life, gathered the crew, came forward and said,

"Everyone gather up! This is a special project, and I need all hands on deck!" I have been waiting for the right time to begin this project, and the time has finally come. First, we must start with demolition. We have to knock down those high walls that have been built up and re-lay a new foundation. Those who have my nurturing, patient heart come forward. Now is when those lessons you learned out of your pain will be put to good use. I told you that I waste nothing!

Show her love and grace throughout this journey of healing. Be patient with her in this chapter of her life called "The Undoing." She is going to need it. Encouragers come forth! I need you to show up when she is ready to throw in the towel. Because it is going to be hard!

While everyone else is tilling her hard ground with love, kindness, patience, grace, correction, and accountability, I will plant seeds. Make sure you rake up every dead root. Dig as deep as possible because I do not want the vultures to snatch the seeds. I want everything fresh and new.

Now, where are the fathers? Ahh, there you are! Come forth. Your role is equally as important. I ask that you represent me the way I have represented myself to you. She hasn't seen this part of me done well. Representing my heart as a father will be vital to her process. Mothers, where are you? Come forth. Nurture her, teach her, and restore her with love and kindness. If you teach her well, she will teach others well."

Oh, what can I say? This is the goodness of God!

"The Lord is gracious and merciful, slow to anger and abounding in steadfast love." See Psalm 145:8 (ESV)

From the time that I arrived from my trip to Ava's, I was an emotional wreck. As I continued to go through the waves of my goodbye, I wondered how long it would be before I regretted my decision and ran back to her as I always did. I don't think I had ever seen myself completely cutting ties with Ava.

Funny enough, this was the week leading into Easter. I didn't have much to do as I didn't do anything related to church. But church was what most folks did on a day like this, so I just decided to do what I knew how to do. I made my way to the east side of town, where all my family lived and often gathered for holidays. I went straight to my aunt's house, and when I arrived, I saw many faces, both familiar and new. The new ones were church folks. Church folks who attended this church that my Godfather had insisted on me visiting.

My Godfather tried to persuade me to attend this church by pointing out that many young people were part of this congregation and that the worship experience was something he believed I would love. Also, I can't forget to mention his emphasis on the possibility of me finding "A good Christian husband who loves the Lord" at this church. In my mind, I couldn't help but roll my eyes and mentally say a sarcastic "bye-boy." I was set on believing that Christian guys were over-spiritual and boring.

Moving on, I made my way to the kitchen, and my primary mission was to grab some ham, *"Arroz con gandules"*- Spanish yellow rice and pigeon peas, and potato salad. Priorities, right?

I engaged in some small talk with familiar faces but kept a safe distance from the church folks. Being around church folks made me nervous; I didn't want them to pull a "Thus Sayeth the Lord" on me.

Many Easter-themed movies were being played on TV, including that good ol' *"The Passion Of The Christ."* This well-known film is known for its raw portrayal and graphic scenes depicting the crucifixion of Jesus Christ. I had watched this movie more times than I could count. But this time, there was a set-up. This time, it was different.

I walked into the living room and found a seat on the couch just in time for the scene where Jesus was getting ready to be crucified. I watched attentively as He endured the mockery and the beatings, still with so much love and compassion in His eyes. How could someone have the strength to endure such intense, agonizing pain for the sake of saving people who didn't want to be saved and loving people who didn't love Him back? None of the idols I served would have ever done what Jesus did for me. If anything, all those false gods ever did was take from me, steal from me, use me, and destroy me in the process. Something was happening inside of me, and every false god I had ever placed on the throne of my heart was being pushed off.

I watched in horror as those Roman soldiers pulled His beard out, spat on Him, placed a crown of thorns on His head, and drove nails into His hands and feet. I could hear Jesus, His voice filled with agony and love, saying, *"I did this for you, even when you would tell me no!"*

It was all becoming so real to me at that moment. I had a head knowledge of this sacrifice, but at that moment, I had a revelation of that sacrifice.

Jesus came down from His throne to die a sinner's death He didn't deserve—but a death I deserved. The crucifixion of Jesus Christ never meant so much to me as it did that day when I watched that scene where He took that beating that would leave those horrifying, painful love lashes on His back—exposing Him in a way that would leave Him unrecognizable and vulnerable in all states. He really became my sin, although He knew no sin so that I could become the righteousness of God. THIS... was real love.

> *"For our sake he made him to be sin who knew no sin, so that in him we might become the righteousness of God."*
> See 2 Corinthians 5:21 (ESV)

God's love was present in that living room, and God's overwhelming love made it difficult to hold on to that "G card "as I tried to hold back the tears. My heart was racing, and the minister I was trying so hard to avoid seemed to sense exactly what was unfolding without saying a single word. Easter, a holiday that was so common and secularized for me, became what it was intended to do. It was my John 3:16 moment. I began to believe.

> *"For God so loved the world that he gave his only begotten son. That whosoever believes in him will not perish but have everlasting life."* John 3:16 (NIV)

I can't remember what led that minister to spark a conversation with me, and I can't remember what was said word for word. But I do remember this one line he said that I hung onto for dear life, "If you want to be delivered, come this Sunday to church, and you will be delivered." How was he so confident that I would get this thing he called deliverance? How was he so sure that I even needed deliverance, for that matter? I had agreed to go to this meeting place where he promised that I would receive freedom.

This minister was kind enough to leave me a friendly tip attached to this life-changing event he had promised I would obtain. He said, "Just prepare yourself because now that you have made this commitment, the enemy will try to stop you."

I couldn't help but to think about what that actually meant. With all that had happened in my life until this point, I didn't want any more smoke! I was grateful for the tip, but the warning didn't lessen the blow. Nonetheless, he was right! That week was hell.

The Beautiful Exchange

In the days leading up to my meeting with Jesus, a heavy sense of guilt about the past and doubts about my decision flooded my thoughts once again. It was like this never-ending replay of memories in my mind, and the nightmares increased and made the anxiety worse. The level of confusion I had was beyond anything I had ever experienced. To top it off, the people I had created unhealthy ties with all popped up during this week. It's crazy how the enemy knows how to make you fall! Yet, as each day passed, I held on to the fact that Sunday was getting closer—I was closer to deliverance day.

The night before, as I was getting ready for the Sunday morning service, there was a mix of excitement and uncertainty about the church I was about to visit. Questions raced through my mind like, "Would I be welcomed? Was I going to leave feeling unchanged? What if this thing called deliverance didn't happen? What if I couldn't be delivered from this?" I could feel the panic bubbling up like it did on a day when I decided to visit this little Methodist church. I remember being desperate for Jesus and equally petrified that He would turn me away.

As I made my way through the foyer of that church, I was greeted with a bright smile and a face that glowed with love. A simple yet welcoming "God bless you" brought so much ease and warmth to my heart that it made the anxiety and fear crumble in a second. I felt the warmth, safety, and authenticity in that small church. I didn't feel judged walking in because my attire was not up to par. It was really all love.

I walked through these double doors that led me into the sanctuary and witnessed the young and the old worshipping with the same intensity and passion. Their hands were raised, eyes closed, some weeping, others praising, but they were all lifting their voices and hands unto the one I was there to meet. In the presence of God, I felt undone and disarmed. I was reminded of the youth services my uncle had invited me to. But this time, as I felt God's presence, I didn't resist. I was ready to surrender and give up the life I was fighting God to keep.

The worship portion of the service had ended, and the sermon began. I remember this young man stepping up to give the word. To my disbelief, he was the senior pastor. He looked so young. I thought he was filling in. But he was really the senior pastor of this church. Then I thought, "Well, we'll see what's up with this kid when he starts preaching." I was surprised by the level of conviction that this young man preached the word of God with. It was then that I was convinced that he was really the senior pastor.

THE MEETING WITH JESUS

He articulated the Father's heart with such depth and clarity that I was able to receive the Gospel in a way that I had never been able to receive it before.

After he was done preaching, there was an altar call, and the worship team made its way up. The lights dimmed again, taking off some of the pressure of being afraid to be vulnerable. I was glad they did this because I was heading towards the ugly cry. People were making their way up to the altar, but I didn't plan to go. I thought it would be something close to the Pentecostal altar calls that always left me more scared than freed. So, I stayed in my seat. I was like, "God, If you want to touch me, you're going to have to do it from here."

"You provide the fire, and I'll provide the sacrifice; you provide the spirit, and I will open up inside. Fill me up God, fill me up God, fill me up God, fill me up."

This is the song they were singing called "Fill Me Up" by Jesus Culture and Kim Walker. I began to weep because that was my prayer. I wanted to be filled with peace, love, and joy. I was crying out to be freed. I was crying out to be healed and delivered. I wanted more than relief. This time I really wanted God.

The time of ministry was ending as almost everyone had been prayed for. But there was still more that I needed to release. Like I needed a little more time. The lights came on anyway, and that meant that the service was coming to an end. I was trying so hard to get myself together before anyone noticed that I had a meltdown in God's presence. At the time, my aunt attended this church, and she was sitting next to me. She turned over and hugged me, and that did it for me. Right in the middle of the hug, everything left came out. The pause button on my tears must've been broken because I couldn't stop crying, and the volume of the cry got louder and louder. I guess this wouldn't be finished at home as I had hoped.

Sensing something was happening, the pastor told the congregation, "Please give reverence to the Holy Spirit; He's still doing something." And they all just waited. They patiently waited until the Holy Spirit was done doing whatever He was doing in me. When I finally stopped crying, I felt a serene presence around me and within me. I was in awe of what had transpired. There was an exchange. A transaction took place. It seemed like nothing grand had occurred on the outside, but I could feel on the inside that something in me had changed forever. Since that day, I have never looked back. I never went back to that relationship, either. It was my new birthday. The day I became a new creation. Deliverance happened.

I made that church my home church. It's where God planted me for the first eleven years of my journey. This is where the Lord met me in profound ways. This was the place where I experienced many seasons of growth and breakthrough. This was the place where I got baptized—in water and fire. In that house, I was loved and graced into and through maturation. This house provided a space for me to discover deep prophetic worship and develop a love for prayer. This church gave me a platform to explore the initial stages of my identity and provided the healing that was necessary for me to move forward. I am eternally grateful for this ministry that opened its doors and hearts to me when I needed it the most. Had I grasped even a little of God's kindness and love towards me, I probably would have run to Him sooner. But I was afraid to relinquish control of my life to God because I didn't trust Him. This mistrust stemmed from a lack of understanding about who Jesus truly was and how I perceived Him as a Father and a savior. I've expressed this in many ways, but God's presence was present even when I couldn't perceive it. I may never fully understand why He continued to graciously interrupt my life with His mercy. Nevertheless, I am grateful for this beautiful exchange.

Section 6

Chapter Twenty

The Transition

I thought that once I embarked on this journey called salvation, it would mark the finish line for all the troubles that came with my past life. I had imagined life looking something like Jesus stepping into the ring after my long, tiresome fight, lifting my tiny, weary arms in triumph, and proudly declaring me the brawl winner! I assumed that from here on out, the only thing I needed to do was to focus on building my new relationship with Christ and that the road would be easy-peasy lemon squeezy. However, I failed to calculate all the new troubles that would attach themselves to my decision. Yes, there is a new life after you accept Jesus, making you a new creation. Yes, you have the victory through Christ Jesus, and you always win, no matter what! Yes, the blood of Jesus is the payment for your sins, but none of these things eliminate the process.

It wasn't long before that champion feeling was gone. If anything, I was starting to feel more like a busted-up Rocky Balboa trying to yell out an "Adrian" while dragging myself through the end of every round of life. *Life was lifing!* I was waiting for Jesus to come out and tell me that I had been punked because this was not what I had in mind when I gave my life to Him.

I thought things would get better instantly; instead, they got worse. The road became even rockier when everything I thought was immovable became movable. Especially after I lost stability once again. The next thing I knew, I was moving out of my apartment, and of all people, I was moving in with my father. I moved in while we still had many unresolved issues. But despite our history, this was the best option then, and I needed a place to stay. Plus, my dad offered, and things were different, right?

One of the first tests during my transition was not even the most obvious, like fixing my potty mouth. Rather, it was learning how to navigate relationships as a new believer with a new set of standards that only applied to me. Choosing to live this lifestyle that was different than everyone else's created a new tension I had never been forced to manage.

Trying to live a life that seemed to be interpreted as "holier than thou" silently increased the tension between my family and me. Especially because they had high expectations and no grace. I would have been more willing to eat a jean jacket instead! There was little time between my conversion as a believer and who they remembered me as, which was the loud, mouthy, and ratchet me that I was still working on disciplining. Sometimes, it felt like it would be impossible to walk this life out without returning to the comfort of my old ways.

It hit me that agreeing to follow Jesus wasn't the hardest part. It was the part where I had to die to self and choose to do things God's way. Doing it

God's way meant I couldn't run to the bar when I was stressed and drink away my sorrows. Doing it God's way meant I couldn't run to my pack of cigarettes, my blunt, or people to destress. Doing it God's way looked a lot like identifying many of those things I deemed as normal that God saw as sinful and cutting them out of my life.

This included friendships, which were with people I deeply loved. Because of my new life in Christ and the things they were still into, our connection naturally weakened, leading us to drift apart or them choosing to distance themselves. We no longer had anything in common. Remember, these people weren't just anybody. These people were there for me when I needed them! But that's the reality of growth – you can't bring everyone along on the journey.

Staying pure was another battle. Do you think it was easy to honor God literally with everything? It wasn't just about controlling my thoughts and attitudes; honoring God with everything extended to my very body! Trying to keep your purity while you keep getting those invites for Netflix and chill ain't for the weak, y'all! That's a different type of self-control. For a little while, it felt like I was suppressing my desires and feelings in exchange for nothing but a couple of goosebumps and emotional cries.

Did I mention that choosing Jesus doesn't always feel good at first? It hurt enough to make me want to quit every single time. But I had tried everything, and Jesus was the only way I had not tried for real. I had to keep reminding myself of what my past decisions and old strategies had gotten me. I couldn't keep running from God because of my frustrations and fear.

Sure, it would have been easier to lower the standards and do it my way. That would mean watering down the Gospel and maybe adding some of my fleshy mixtures to make it more attainable and tasteful. But it always seems like the bitter medicine does the job. This is not something that can be attained through the flesh. It requires God's Spirit to carry it out. *Come on, somebody!*

I had to let go of everything familiar, comfortable, and satisfying to the flesh. I had to recognize that the things I thought were healing me were only making me sicker. Although I felt like I was losing, Matthew 16:25 (NIV) reminded me of this:

"For whoever wants to save their life will lose it, but whoever loses their life for me will find it."

Yes, it felt like I had lost my life—or should I say what I thought was life? But I found it in Christ. And no, it isn't as boring as I believed. If anything, there is more joy in this than in all the worldly experiences I had once considered joyful.

To be transparent, bringing the flesh under the submission of Christ was not something I mastered every single time. Corinthians 10:13 had to become real to me through this time of purging and sanctification. And this verse sealed everything I had been feeling the pressure of with a promise! That He would always make a way out, and just like Jesus Himself had been tempted in every way and overcame, I, too, could overcome because He overcame!

The initial sanctification process I experienced was only for a season; as we know, seasons don't last forever. After enduring this lengthy season of stripping, weeding out, and pruning, I now understand why it had to be done this way. Without this agonizing process, there simply wouldn't have been another way to bring me to where I needed to be. Let me let you in on a secret. Processes are inevitable and cannot be avoided, skipped, or shortened. But the benefits that come with the process will far outweigh what might seem like never-ending trials. The process will yield results, bear fruit, and shape your character.

I think back on it now, and oh, how I remember those many days and nights when I cried out of frustration because I couldn't understand why the process had to be so hard. I never got direct answers from God as to why. As life unfolded, I no longer needed to ask God why. I saw the why. Let's just say God is a good Father, and He knows what He's doing. He knows how to take care of His children.

The storms of life left the soil of my heart dry, barren, and incapable of nurturing anything fresh and new. Therefore, God had to start over and that was a painful crushing. Yet, through all of this, I am sure of this: had God permitted even a single tie to my past, if I had any other options besides Jesus Himself, I would've compromised and returned to my old ways in a heartbeat. Pain can be turned into purpose.

Now, I find myself delicately nurtured and tended by THE Master Gardener, who has transformed my life into a masterpiece through designs forged in the fires of trials. I'm thankful that He didn't stop loving the HELL out of me! Pun intended. I am grateful that He vigorously worked my ground no matter what it took and no matter how much it hurt, no matter how many times I begged Him to stop.

Here I am, twelve years later, living in the fruit of that moment. Because of His goodness, kindness, mercy, and correction, I have evolved into the woman I had always aspired to be. The person I have become surpasses the vision of who I had ever dreamed of becoming. My idea of what a healthy version of myself should've looked like was incredibly weak compared to who I have evolved into. My faith at the time only stretched as far as envisioning a life involving necessities, moments of joy, and survival. I can boldly say that I am who I am today because of an "Only God" accomplishment. I never had the faith to see the life I am currently living. Sometimes, I still can't believe I ended up being as blessed as I am. This attitude of gratitude begins with my husband.

I have been married to my best friend for eleven years. Yes, as cheesy as it sounds, he is my best franddddd! Okay! He is a God-fearing man who also happens to be handsome. And to think I believed I couldn't get both. He loves the Lord just like my Godfather said a Godly man should. He is a laid-down lover of Christ and is everything ... but corny. Thank you, Jesus! He constantly fills our home with joy and laughter. Sometimes, with so much of it, I have been pretty close to peeing my pants more than a few times—pre-babies at that. Only mama bears would understand what that's like.

I know how I describe my happy ending may seem like it's too good to be true. Something most would say is not real life. But it is real life. What you see is what you get. Does it mean that our marriage is perfect? No, not at all. We are flawed in many ways. I mean, come on, I am Puerto Rican. By nature, we are a little crazy. But marriage was used as a means of healing. Marriage healed me.

Together, we have faced unpredictable circumstances. Together, we have confronted difficult seasons that involved sickness and financial struggles. Marriage has forced us to learn how to navigate internal issues that had nothing to do with one another. We have had to fight through it all to be where we are at now. Through it all, we had to train our eyes to see beauty in every circumstance. Even the ones that were downright scary.

Within this training ground called marriage, God has allowed me to learn so many lessons I would not have been able to learn elsewhere. The opportunity to grow my faith was found within this marriage after a bad doctor's report said that the Multiple Sclerosis my husband was diagnosed with at the age of thirteen was progressing. We had to contend to believe the opposite no matter what we saw. By the way, he did pull through. By the grace of God, he defies all the odds.

Marriage has taught me how to communicate effectively in situations that seemed to be the perfect occasion for me to go off! This is where God showed me to me. This is where the motives of my heart were exposed, and the things I called "triggers" began to reveal their roots. Through this, I could see the worst parts of me that were created through trauma that I didn't even know I was still dealing with. But because I love God and I love my husband, I chose to heal. The exposure made me feel bare, but it allowed me to heal. God will reveal what He desires to heal.

Marriage has been my teacher in humility. It's where I've learned to set aside my pride and own my junk. We've learned to apologize even when feels uncomfortable. Many opportunities were given to learn how to give and receive grace. Again, all this was found in the trenches of marriage. I have understood this one thing: when the motive is love, it can empower you to do all things. Love really covers a multitude of sins. See 1 Peter 4:8.

Together, we have a ten-year-old daughter and an eight-year-old son, who are literal, splitting images of ourselves. My son is my McDreamy, hazel-eyed baby boy who is a ball of energy whose only motivation is to give his momma lots of kisses, remind me of every promise I made, and use all the corrections I use with him against me. He is always ready for sword fights and can snack out of my cupboards until I'm broke. Meanwhile, my daughter is the opposite except for the snack part. She is calm, graceful, tender, gentle, spontaneous, adventurous, creative, and brave. She is my curly top twin. She constantly fills me in with all the Snapple cap, miscellaneous facts that have ever existed, and all the summaries of the "Who What Show" episodes. Together, they keep me sharp and tired all at the same time. Most days, I'm running on lots of espresso and prayer. Whatever the cost, I love them in a way I never thought I could love another human being. It's that "no matter what" kind of love.

Parenthood has been one of the most incredible opportunities to learn who God is as a Father. It has shown me the tender parts of God's heart as a Father and the depth of His love for me through my children. I think of my position and assignment as a mother, and I can't ever see myself being angry at my child forever. As a mother, I want my children to know that I love them every second of every day, no matter what. As a mother, I want my children to know I am accessible. Likewise, God, as a Father, wanted me to know He felt like this about me, too. I parent my children how God parents me, and I have learned to love them how God loves me.

How do children learn to be so forgiving? How do they learn to be so merciful? It's God's heart deposited in these little ones. I remember being pregnant, and I felt the weight of the responsibility that would come with my new role as a mother. Not only the pressure that came with caring for them but also the pressure that comes with raising them in the ways of the Lord. But little did I know that they had as much purpose in being my babies as I did in being their momma bear. They were a part of God's divine strategy to get me to understand how He loves me and how I could learn to love back.

Along with the amazing family I have gained, I have had the privilege to experience beautiful friendships that have shaped my life for the better. These friendships were also a vital part of my healing journey. Although our paths have changed as we have gone in different directions, I will always be grateful for these two women who remained constant during the difficult seasons of my life.

As a kid, I loved watching this show called "The Golden Girls." I wondered how these women managed to live with each other despite their clashing personalities, constant disagreements about their life choices, and more. Yet, they were still present, loving, and forbearing toward one another.

How were they able to love each other so well? Well, they were friends, but they were soul sisters. They had something integrated within their dynamic that was real enough to trailblaze through anything thrown at them. I had never seen this demonstrated healthily in my relationships before these two women came into my life. However, because of these friendships, I understand how.

I believe that the only reason we experienced such a braided, tight friendship is because of the ingredients we chose to integrate into our foundation. I like to compare these ingredients to the Sofrito of your friendship. If you don't have it, it just ain't right, sis! Our sofrito consisted of vulnerability, trust, loyalty, accountability, mercy, transparency, and lots and lots of grace and forgiveness. We were willing to learn to be all these things during our season of friendship, which brought on this tight-knit. As I mentioned, marriage and parenthood were necessary for my healing and maturation, but friendship was equally important.

They taught me beyond the bond of friendship. They taught me things in the place of a mother. These women mothered me through some tough stuff in my life that I probably wouldn't have allowed anyone else to do. They taught me how to be a good wife, serve my husband well, and serve my family joyfully. These were the only women I would allow to see the imperfect parts of me without the fear of judgment. They walked me into the beginning stages of becoming a Godly woman.

Even though I became a mom before them, without reservation, they walked me through motherhood through their own victories and failures. I remember when I just had my son, and I was struggling with the thought of not being able to love my children equally. I know it sounds ridiculous, but it was a real thing. I desperately wanted to be a good mom and not fail. The thought of not knowing how to love my babies uniquely freaked me out. This feeling led me into a conversation with one of these women in my bathroom, where I was crying hysterically. The only thing that kept me hopeful was a simple sentence with a powerful instruction that carried me, "Carmen, ask God to stretch your heart; it's going to be okay. I love you." These are memories that will last a lifetime.

You know, women tend to have reputations when it comes to being catty. That stereotype has long been shattered. You can have healthy relationships with other women that don't involve envy or strife. You can have relationships with other women who know how to respect and honor you as a person. You can love the best parts of someone and not get hung over the ONE thing they can't get right. Granted, not everyone's ONE thing is tolerable, but you still can choose love.

Collectively, through all my experiences with singleness, marriage, friendships, and motherhood, I know what restoration is supposed to look like! I know what healthy relationships are supposed to look and feel like. I know what loving myself and others is supposed to be like.

Are You Delivered?

To my next point, as I'm sure you're wondering: Am I free from same-sex attraction? Free, as in completely free? Free from thoughts, desires, and urges? I will further explain this, beginning with this:

I know who I am and who I am not. Because of this, when the thought comes, if it comes, I can quickly identify its root and amputate that thing without hesitation. Above that, I find myself in a place where I am so satisfied with what I have in my relationship in its entirety that I don't have a longing for what I used to be, what I used to have, or the wandering mind that dives into what could've been. What I have with my husband is as good as it gets, and I am not out searching for what's better. I have the best portion cut out for me, and I am satisfied with that.

Some will mistakenly believe that the evidence of my freedom from a homosexual lifestyle is my marriage and family. It goes way beyond just marriage and children. The fruit of my freedom is found in my life as a whole, not just in my sexuality. Because when God starts something, his intention is always to finish the work.

Freedom began in the God encounter that birthed the shift. It wasn't just about applying practical things like abstaining from sexual immorality. It was much more than that. I made sure to stay close to God, holding on to Him for dear life because this process was so difficult. That allowed me to accept and understand how my choices broke His heart rather than focusing on how uncomfortable I felt about crucifying my flesh. Through intimacy, God exposed the deep-seated issues that were manifesting into lust. He first began healing the little girl in me who had experienced the violation. Then, He peeled back all the layers of perversion that were hiding behind the trauma. There were quite a few of these sessions with the Lord that exposed a whole lot, even things I had forgotten about.

As I continued to seek Him through the cravings, I began to want Him more than the very sin I once was in love with. Now, I don't want to be insensitive in saying that most people who are struggling are folks who just don't want to be free. But I do believe that if you want it, it is available. But more so, the question is, how free do you want to be? Are you willing to adjust, leave, and separate, if need be, to obtain your freedom?

I believe that what kept me from freedom was believing that God would have never been able to give me anything better than what I had. I believed that if I surrendered all, including my sexuality, I would be settling for a mediocre life, having salvation, but I would be miserable. I will say, because

I'm now on the other side of this, God does not take your brokenness to give you brokenness. He takes your brokenness and seals it with refined gold. You always look better than how you came.

If this happens to be up your alley, where you find yourself hesitant to surrender because you can't fathom what life would be like after, here is my advice. I know it feels scary just to start over. I know it can even feel impossible to envision a life outside of what has always been. But it is possible, and you will make it if you allow him to walk you through it.

Wouldn't you want to know God way beyond your deliverance? It's way beyond that one miracle in your life. Your pursuit of him is much more than just getting free and securing your seat in heaven. It's about restoring your relationship with the Father and entering into your God-given identity as first, daughter, or son. I know that these straightforward statements seem like they are much easier said than done. I know this! I have been there. Remember that I walked through this, too, so I can speak to this! And because I know how difficult it can be, I want to provide you with some tips that helped me through this journey of freedom, healing, and discovery of identity. I pray this will help you along your journey as much as it helped me throughout mine.

1. Get to the Root

Getting to the root may require you to seek deep counsel to understand what false truths you have believed about yourself and God. Undoing these lies will open your eyes to many things. Like why you may be wired the way you're wired. What keeps you stuck in that same place, unable to move forward? At times, it's shame that clings onto you and makes you believe that this thing has stained your record. Or it may be the fear of what people may say about you. Whatever it may be, exposing the root will help you to understand the why. Then, you can execute the "how" full throttle. You may have to go really deep and really far back. You might have to renounce some things and even go as far back into the 3rd and 4th generations to renounce things that maybe your ancestors did. This is found in Exodus 34:7 (KJV), which says,

> *"God "[visits] the iniquity of the fathers on the children and the children's children, to the third and the fourth generation."*

This just means that there may be some things you are dealing with that probably don't have anything to do with you. It may just be in the bloodline- Generational curses. But the deeper you go, the more you will discover. It may even surprise you. This step may come across the table once you are ready to go through an actual deliverance. It may be an inner soul healing or further than that. In addition, make a conscious decision to abandon every justification to keep loving your sin so that you can fully embrace what the Lord wants to do in your life. Kill the resistance with your pursuit!

2. Be Intentional

Be intentional about everything! Be intentional about staying away from certain types of environments. Whether or not you're there by choice or accident. Be intentional about the conversations you're engaging in. I can't stress this enough: *BE INTENTIONAL!* I am not saying you must bury yourself in a cave and hide from everyone forever. But don't put yourself in a situation where you know you may fall. This is where boundaries are important and necessary. As we know, boundaries are not a bad thing. They keep you healthy and safe and define the limit for others and yourself.

There will be some who will not respect this and purposely misunderstand you. They may even cut you off suddenly with no explanation. It comes with the territory. My advice... Baby, grow some tough skin! Prepare yourself for the chatter because this walk is not for the faint of heart! But it will develop your character like nothing else in your life will. Prayer will always be the thing that sustains you through anything that comes with change, especially when God is the one telling you to shift. But there are some practical things you can do that don't take a prophetic word and *shadaboughtahonda* tongue-talking prayer for you to do. Baby, what you do is block, delete, and swerve! Now, I will say this: brace yourself. This will be a frustrating season. It will feel like you're starting over, and it's... because you are! That's why this next tip is just as important as this one.

3. Get Plugged Into a Church Community

You may have to visit a few of these before you feel like you have arrived at a place where you may be ready to settle in. This may be a place that's your forever home or a home for a season. Either way, the body is a good place to start connecting with people who can help you along your journey. You need the entire body to function well so you can function well. Finding someone who has overcome this very thing you're up against can be a testimony to fuel your drive.

There are several ways to identify a good, spirit-filled church community. Some are disputable, but the doctrine is not! Sound doctrine is not a debatable matter. They gotta preach what's in the word and its context—nothing more and nothing less. A good, healthy body is not only a community that provides sound doctrine. It's also a body that offers safe and healthy fellowship and discipleship. You need both. I had visited a few church communities before I found the place where I felt like I was at home. Once I did, I kept myself plugged in by attending their main services along with whatever fellowship gatherings were available—including but not limited to prayer nights, Bible studies, and women's nights. I also incorporated a few online churches.

At the beginning of my walk, Pastor Jentzen Franklin played a huge role in opening my eyes to many things I was completely unaware of. It helped to make sense of my process and gave me hope in this newfound life in Christ. I don't call him Pastor Jentzen Franklin anymore; I call him Grandpa Jentzen. One day, I'm going to meet him. But I would watch plays that he had out on YouTube called "Spirit of the Python," "Warning Signs." and "Keep your underwear on." These plays opened my eyes to the spiritual realm and allowed me to be more conscious of what was happening when I made certain decisions.

Remember that leaving any lifestyle with its own community may leave you feeling like you are outside the camp. That may bring on loneliness and make you want to go back. Listen to me! Let me encourage you! You got this! God has got you! Hold on! You will find your tribe!

4. Accountability

This is a huge one! Please pray about who this person is, even if you are a new believer and may not know exactly what you need and how you must pray about this. Just ask God to show you who. God knows who this is. He knows what you need even before you ask. See Matthew 6:8. This person must preferably be a seasoned believer and can't be someone who is struggling with what you're trying to get out of. Now, prepare yourself because you will be uncomfortable. No doubt about that! But it will be beneficial. You need someone who is going to challenge you, someone who's going to check you. Someone who is going to tell you the truth even when it hurts. Sometimes, you need the shepherd's rod.

Also, ask the Holy Spirit to help you become teachable. You can't help someone who doesn't want to be helped, and you can't teach someone who is unteachable and thinks they know everything. In this accountability thing, you will, at times, feel offended. Remember, God's word is offensive when you are defending your sin. I know this too well. So remember not to make your accountability partner your enemy when they are correcting you. Don't wallow in your mistakes when you realize you made one. Just repent, fix it, and move on.

> "And we know that all things work together for good to those who love God, to those who are called according to His Purpose."
> Romans 8:28 (KJV)

5. Intimacy

I cannot stress this enough! Intimacy will be the very thing that sustains you and grows you. This is the source. This is where the transformation happens. This is where you find your identity. This is where you are renewed. This is where oil is produced.

Intimacy with the Lord can be as simple as reading your word. I run into people all the time who tell me they want to know about God; they want to learn the voice of God. They want to know God's will over their lives. But they don't know anything about Him. They don't know His character; they don't know His ways, and they don't understand His principles. The most disappointing part is that this language comes from people who have been in the walk for years. If you don't read the word, how can you identify the difference between a good thing and a God thing? How else would you be able to distinguish between the voice of God and the voice of the enemy? Get in your word!

Spending time with the Lord doesn't look the same for everyone, but it is important to converse with Him in your day. Sometimes, it can look like unspoken prayer, soaking in His presence and letting Him speak to you. But without intimacy with the Lord, you won't make it, and this will be pure religion. It would feel more like behavior modification and not a life transformation. You will frustrate yourself striving and wear yourself out!

While the practical methods I used to stay free may differ, and the ways God brought me through may also vary, the goal remains unchanged. Be intentional about your purity, keep the fire burning, and always remember to grow, grow, grow!

Chapter Twenty-One

Mom... We Will Keep Trying

Have you ever been hurt so deeply by someone that, despite knowing forgiveness is the right thing to do, you are unable to grant it? It's almost like the offense was too great to overlook. Oh man, do I know someone who has struggled with this, and boy, do I know them very well. Side note: It's me. I am that someone! Countless times, I felt authorized not to forgive. But the Bible is very clear on the stance of forgiveness. You forgive so that you may be forgiven.

> *"But if you do not forgive men their trespasses, neither will your father forgive you."* Matthew 6:15 (KJV)

God is so serious about us choosing forgiveness that if you don't forgive, it delays answered prayers.

"If I regard iniquity in my heart, the Lord will not hear."
Psalms 66:18 (KJV)

Beyond an unanswered prayer, it is scientifically proven that it can make you sick. Unforgiveness increases anxiety and causes depression, high blood pressure, heart disease, and so much more. There are countless articles and documentaries that validate this statement. To take it a step further, God is so serious about us choosing forgiveness that He will instruct you to leave whatever you have brought for Him as a gift at the altar so that you can resolve the issue with your brother first.

23 *"Therefore, if you are offering your gift at the altar and there remember that your brother or sister has something against you,* **24** *leave your gift there in front of the altar. First, go and be reconciled to them; then come and offer your gift.* Matthew 5: 23-24 (NIV)

We look at Jesus, who displayed boundless forgiveness despite experiencing the worst betrayals by those who claimed they loved Him. How could He forgive and love them as if nothing had ever happened? It sounds too good to be true. It's more like a job that only Jesus can do. Ironically enough, true forgiveness is a job that only Jesus can enable you to do.

Forgiveness does not come easily, as it is not always the initial response to offense. Why? Because forgiveness comes after your pride. Furthermore, the act of forgiveness forces you to relinquish control and entitlement. Unforgiveness and offense are rooted in pride, and forgiveness lies in the opposite of pride—humility. When you choose forgiveness, it never means you're excusing the behavior or the act. Choosing forgiveness simply says,

"Lord, I will let you handle this. I trust you with my pain, I trust you to heal me from this, and I trust that you will make something good out of this."

Consider the story of Joseph, as recounted in the book of Genesis. He was a man who, through his God-given gift, ultimately saved an entire nation during a period of famine. Now ask me, how on earth did he end up in Egypt at just the right time in the first place? Hmm, good question. Through betrayal! God allowed him to leverage a disadvantage, like a betrayal, into an opportunity for growth and development. This led him to step into his God-given assignment, which led him straight into purpose and restored his relationship with his family. So, remember this story whenever you think about how someone has wronged you. God will work it out for your good.

"You intended to harm me, but God intended it for good to accomplish what is now being done, the saving of many lives.
Genesis 50:20 (NIV)

Although the benefits of forgiving are great in the long run, the sentiments attached to the act of the offense don't always go away instantly. Ruminating thoughts about what they did will play a role in your emotions if you let it. But if your heart is positioned towards God and your desire to do the will of the Father is at the forefront, he will help you get there. I add that reconciliation doesn't always come with forgiveness, either. Many mistake forgiveness with immediate restoration. Although, I am confident that it is always in the Lord's will to bring reconciliation. Unfortunately, it doesn't always turn out that way. It could be for many reasons that have much to do with the individuals, or it could be that the season is over. But at times, all that will be left after that release will be lessons learned and the choice to heal.

The process of forgiveness and healing comes in different stages as well. As I had mentioned, I have struggled with grief that is not associated with physical death. In my experience, grief has been attached to accepting that things will be different, that what was—no longer exists, and that there isn't anything you can do about it. Welcoming this "new normal" will trigger other emotions like anger, and if not checked, it may open a window for bitterness. And oh, how the enemy loves to play with our emotions to plant seeds and keep us yoked to anything that isn't like Jesus. Sadly, this is where I got stuck many years ago with my mom.

I held my mother hostage to our past. I felt authorized to do so as a punishment for how I felt she had failed me as her daughter. I found myself triggered by things she would say, even in responses that were unrelated to me, but these responses echoed our past. Although I acknowledged that healing was needed, I believed healing could only begin once she changed. Notice how I said, "until she changed." I'll unpack that a little later.

We had a history filled with so many "I can't believe it" moments that the history kept my resistance and resentment running strong. I wasn't willing to throw away the files just because some progress had popped up from time to time. I was not impressed with a little bit of progress. I needed to see that the patterns were non-existent in order for me to move forward. But when I saw that the patterns were still present and that they kept leading me into the same kind of disappointments, it built that wall up a little bit higher every time—this is fortified unforgiveness.

There were so many other signs that flashed brightly, identifying my unforgiveness. It just wasn't something that I could identify right away. Mostly because my definition of unforgiveness was narrowed down to the more toxic ways it's displayed. I figured I was working through this, so I wasn't struggling with unforgiveness. Despite what I believed, my definition did not constrain all that this rotten emotion was intended to do and what it was already doing in my life. It was stealing my joy, peace, health, and all the blessings assigned to me. It had become a blockage, a ceiling that capped my next level.

A few years into my walk, there was a period where I began to realize that this thing between my mother and me was a lot more serious than I had perceived. How did I know? Well, it was the one thing that the Holy Spirit kept digging his finger into. The Holy Spirit began to make me hyper-aware of our dysfunction and how I handled my mother. Suddenly, I crossed over from seeing our relationship struggles as a nuisance to a conviction. It was like the Holy Spirit had placed His lens over my eyes, examining us through God's standards. I began to see the disconnect between what I preached and how I felt. This was all placed under God's magnifying glass during an experience I had in 2018, in the days leading to Yom Kippur, during a time of consecration.

I entered into prayer and began with thanksgiving, my usual practice. Suddenly, I thought, "I should thank the Lord for my parents." This thought took me back a bit because I often prayed for my parent's well-being and that they would be whole in Christ, but I rarely expressed gratitude for them without any particular reason. Nonetheless, I proceeded.

I started with small acknowledgments, thanking God that they provided shelter, food, etc. It felt anything but organic to hear myself say these things. I continued expressing gratitude towards other things they had done that I had somehow overlooked. Things that could have made life harder had they not done THAT ONE thing right. In the middle of that, I was so overwhelmed by what I was saying that I began to weep bitterly, crying out of conviction. There was something about hearing myself acknowledging their efforts that made me realize that I still had anger and unforgiveness toward them.

I was quickly drawn into a vision where the Lord revealed the true condition of my heart and, even more so, the condition of my mother's heart. Granted, God wasn't excusing all that happened by bringing me conviction. He was addressing the condition of my heart because I was a believer, I knew better, and I was held to a higher standard. Most importantly, it was about what this unforgiveness was doing to me.

The vision was in black and white. It resembled that of a vintage era. I found myself in the middle of a well-known strip, surrounded by a crowd circling something that had everyone's attention. People were hopping over each other to see what was happening. I could hear the people talking about what was taking place. I could hear the vintage cameras flashing as they captured these moments. I pushed through the crowd to make it into the inner circle. There, I saw a person on the ground trying to cover their face from cameras and onlookers, leaving them with no room to run or hide. Immediately, I became angry with this mean paparazzi crew because they showed no remorse. "What an injustice?" I thought.

Then, I saw an old newspaper spiraling quickly, similar to how old TV announcements would appear. When it finally stopped, I knew that the photo that made the headlines was the one taken by the paparazzi. The front cover of that paper was a person on the ground covering their face with their hands. If the paper had a headline, this cover would suggest humiliation.

Instantly, I knew the person in that picture, the one I had looked upon with compassion over the injustice, was my mother. I felt her shame, her guilt, and her pain as she had been exposed in such a way, leaving her defenseless. With so much regret, I thought, "Oh, my goodness, I am the mean paparazzi who left her no room to escape her past mistakes." At that moment, the Lord firmly told me,

"Stop taking your mother's mistakes and putting them on the front page. You will never have to sacrifice what she had to sacrifice, and you won't ever have to endure the hardships she had to endure. You feel like she didn't give you anything when she gave you everything. She gave you the best thing in your life. She gave you me."

As He spoke, I continued to see pictures of all she had gone through—things related to her childhood and her relationship with my father. I saw glimpses of everything she did that I saw as common and began to see them as the grand sacrifices that they were. I was completely unaware of the price she paid daily to stay afloat. I understood what He meant with every rebuke He spoke into my spirit. I can't tell you how I knew; I just knew! Allow me to clarify: this book is not an exposure. Back then, when I spoke about the things that affected me, I did it from a hurt place. I never considered what she went through and why she did what she did. My recount of our story then did not involve redemption, love, and grace. It only involved my pain.

Through my vision, I could see and acknowledge things I had overlooked about my mother because of my pain. This encounter allowed me to realize that my mother had also been a victim of many things that had trickled down into our relationship as mother and daughter. You see, my mother had experienced numerous tragedies in her own life, many that only God could heal her from. It was challenging to empathize with her because I had been viewing her through the lens of a child in need of her mommy. This lens made me see myself as the only victim. When the Lord allowed me to see her through the lens of a mother and through His eyes, it hit differently. I began to see the little girl in her also crying out to be rescued. It brought on a deeper level of compassion for her. For once, I didn't see the woman who failed me. I saw a woman who did her best with what she had. I saw the woman God loved just as much as He loved me. At that moment, the Lord healed the mommy wound in me and brought me to where I was supposed to be.

I am so grateful for the conviction because I was allowing my pain to become an excuse not to get well. After this encounter, I began to see breakthroughs in other areas of my life as I chose to walk in forgiveness. Even my intimacy with God grew. Seeing God's heart in this way reassured me that He could be trusted. I was then able to release that rugged, halyard rope of trauma from my bloody and bruised hands. When I gave my life to the Lord, I stepped into this relationship with Christ as a sinner needing a savior. But learning about forgiveness of self and others led me into a journey of discovering my identity in Christ. I was learning not to identifyas an orphan, but rather to identify as daughter who has been adopted into the family of God. The process of forgiveness that God walked me through allowed Him to work not only on me but also on my mom. I never realized I was her accuser, keeping her tied to all those rotten roots by reminding her of her wrongs in spiteful ways. In other words, my unresolved pain set her healing back, too.

This shift abolished those unrealistic expectations I had set for my mother, and I was no longer comparing our relationship to what it should have looked like. I wasn't looking for opportunities to remind her of her failures. I also wasn't waiting for her to change into what I wanted her to be. I had accepted that God was her maker, and He was the only one who could bring change.

It wasn't enough to just forgive. I also had to learn how to honor my mother regardless of our history, even if she had not changed. I had to uphold my duty and responsibility as a believer to honor her without making any more excuses not to do so. Uffff, that was a struggle! I had no idea how to do that! I have learned to honor my mother through my submission to the Holy Spirit. I had to learn to esteem her because of her position and not our past. I had to love her as an adult and not through the heart of that abandoned child.

Honor started slow but became steady. You might ask, "Well, what does honoring your mother look like after all these years?" Well, it looks like small steps that lead into giant ones. It's as simple as making phone calls on birthdays and random calls only to check in. It looks like being kind without expecting something in return. It looks like being intentional about my interaction with her during holidays. It looks like helping her with my resources when I can and choosing to forgive and forget easily. It becomes easier to do this without expectations as I honor her out of love and not obligation.

Our relationship has improved significantly over the years, but that only happened when I shifted my mindset. After a few years of practicing this, can I say I always get it right? Can I say that she gets it right every time? No way! Do we still have disagreements from time to time? Absolutely! But when we reach those points, I'm not allowing the trauma of the past to tear down and undo everything God walked me through. Nor am I choosing to victimize myself, as it is so easy to do. We have our moments; we choose forgiveness and love and then move on. It doesn't always feel that simple or come in that order, but as long as we are both willing, we will keep trying. Mommy, we will keep trying!

Chapter Twenty-Two

Dad... It's Goodbye for Now, but Not Forever

As for my dad, unfortunately, I can't say the same. There have been moments where there was some momentum in the rekindling, but sadly, they were short-lived. I can go down the list of everything I have attempted to do to tip the scales. Beginning with simple things like showing up at his job with coffee, a gift card, and my daughter in a car seat to make a loud statement. I prioritized acknowledging him on birthdays and important family holidays, trying to make them as memorable as possible for both of us. I even invited him into my home many times and hosted him the best way I knew how. You name it, I have done it. He would kindly accept the gifts. He would be a little warmer and more civil than usual. He would say thank you, smile, and maybe sneak in a hug, and that would be the end until I tried again. This cycle continued for years until one year, the rejection hit differently.

It was my 31st birthday, which landed at the beginning of the pandemic. Besides the worldwide chaos, social distancing, and everyday activities that were once available pre-pandemic, it was still a great birthday. For one, I was alive, and we were healthy even after being hit by the first wave. My kids surprised me with gifts and cards, and my husband surprised me with gifts to Ulta. (*That is a big thing for us makeup geeks. If you know, then you know*!) My friends made me a birthday song. I had a Zoom call with all my friends and family! It was great!

But still, something was missing—something like that call and or text I wanted from my dad. I wanted to see something, anything that assured me that all that effort I had put in wasn't for nothing. The year prior, I made the most effort to connect with my father in hopes that something would change. I can't say there was a significant change in our relationship. However, it had been the most change I had seen in over a decade between us. He couldn't have been acting this whole time to then purposely let me down so hard like this again. Nonetheless, the day came and went, and there wasn't a call, a text, or even a generic Happy Birthday Facebook shout-out. *Nada*!

About three days afterward, I still felt the sting of not receiving a birthday acknowledgment. I had felt like this before, but it was more intense this time than any other time. I was thinking of all the times I had with my dad, everything that I had done, all the risks that I had taken, and still, I was being rejected all over again. "How do I get over this again?" I thought. The more serious question was, "Why was I getting all knotted up if I knew what to expect?" As my thoughts continued to ruminate, I just broke down. Again, for the millionth time in my life, about the same disappointment. I remember going into the bedroom where my husband had been working. I sat on the bed with a very somber look. I waited for him to be available, and with a crying shriek, I said, "Babe, I need to talk to you." He turned the chair over and said, "Shoot!" What came out of me began with more of a word-vomit conversation, filled with pain, questions, confusion, and rejection.

"Babe, I am still hurt that my dad didn't call me. How do you just forget that it is your daughter's birthday? I know that's how he is, but why does he keep giving me mixed signals? Why do I have to keep going through this over and over again? Why is he like that towards me? What could I have done to him that hurt him so badly? I know he is hard to love, and I have tried to love him through that, too!"

I know that sounds kind of emotionally unstable. But that is exactly how it came out. I paused and then cried some more. My husband said nothing. He just listened and waited for me to get everything out! I took a deep breath and shifted gears as I continued to air out to my husband.

"All I've wanted to do is gain access! But his behavior is wrong and inexcusable! I don't deserve this! I want him to get it right! I really do, but he is not ready. And I cannot continue doing this at the expense of my heart! Not anymore, at least! I am putting up the yellow tape! I can't change him, no matter what I do! That task is a God thing! I have been trying to prove to him for the longest that I can love him well! That I have changed. That I am willing to work through the stuff we need to work through!"

As I paused to sob, my husband waited, and I could tell that he was looking at me with so much compassion as a father. My husband has seen me dealing with this for as long as we have been together—coping with these very same emotions every holiday, every time my kids had a birthday and there was no call or response, and sometimes even a straight decline to the invitation. But I would see him present for others in the very same way I had requested him to be there for my family. What I realized is that I wasn't as healed as I thought I was. What I wanted from my father was something he wasn't ready to give me. While wiping the tears off my face, with a long sigh, I continued telling my husband,

"I have to create boundaries for myself. They might be invisible to him, but they are visible to me. I can't accept the terms of his relationship with me. It's too painful for me right now. No, I am not going to stop praying for him. No, I am not going to stop loving him. Yes, I would do what I can when there is a need, regardless of how he feels about me or how I feel about him. And I don't know if this is the right thing forever. I just know it is the right thing for right now. I need to heal."

I was at peace about my decision but battled the thought of possibly reacting out of pain and rejection. Could it have been that my emotions were in high gear, and I was making an emotional decision? Wondering if this was a God thing or a me thing, I had a dream just a few days later that brought the clarity and answers I needed to move forward.

In this dream, I found myself in my father's house when he was having a disagreement about someone he had a fallout with. While speaking with him about the disagreement, I addressed his behavior. I told him, "You are wrong about that. That is not how you should've handled this!" His response was very familiar, similar to how he usually responded to me about all disagreements. He was trying to justify his actions by saying, "Well, this is how I am!" His body language and response again felt familiar, mirroring how he harshly dealt with me. The difference is that this time, I was the one on the outside looking in. There was a pause in the dream, almost like everything stood still as I was in deep thought, putting the pieces together. It dawned on me that how he behaved towards me had nothing to do with me and everything to do with how he was. I woke up, knowing this was a dream God had given me. He reassured me that how my father handled me was not my fault. It just happened to be more of a traumatic experience because I was his daughter.

Although having a healthy relationship is what I desire, I choose to heal and choose forgiveness first. While I don't know if time and space will be enough to get our relationship to what it's "supposed" to look like, I know that this is what I need right now. I know that my father's freedom is not contingent on my endurance level or ability to practice long-suffering. Holding on while falling apart will not fix him; holding on while tearing apart will only destroy me. I am sure that a time will come when my compassion will outweigh my disappointment. Where my healing will not allow these "right now" kinds of truths to change how I view myself or even how I love him. It can sometimes feel like everything I had ever tried to do to make things right between us was a waste of my time.

However, I understand that not all sacrifices come with immediate benefits. So even if I can't see the fruit of my actions to make us right, I know that he still saw Jesus in me, which makes it worth it. And even if all those turning-the-cheek moments felt pointless and humiliating, I know nothing is wasted.

I have realized, after much time, that my father's offense is not just personal to me; it's personal to God. And if God can choose to forgive him, then God can enable me to forgive fully, too. But right now, I have to heal to be whole. So, because I desire healing and wholeness more than a result, I know I have to let him go for a little while so I can love him better later. So, until then, it's goodbye for now but not forever!

Chapter Twenty-Three

Its Beauty for Ashes

The idea of my life becoming a book was just a spurt of creativity during a conversation with my husband. Then, boom! Four years later, after that conversation, it became a reality. I would have never thought I would share such intimate details of my life with the world in this format. I can imagine that this is why Jesus had to send more encouragement than I can remember. I can just see it: Jesus in heaven, with His palm to his face for the gazillionth time, like, "*Send another messenger to Carmen, aka Thomas the doubter Jr. Thank you*!" I doubted over and beyond. The closest thing I had ever done to a book was a laminated, colored pencil illustration with a rigid plastic spiral ring in the 3rd grade. I got nominated for it, but still, this is different. So trust me when I say that I would have been A' ok if the closest thing to a book was a journal entry meant for my eyes only.

Nevertheless, the book is here! You are reading through the evidence of my acceptance of the assignment. However, while this was in formation, I struggled with obeying what the Lord had requested of me, mainly because of fear—fears I never knew ran so deep until I was challenged to do something in this capacity simply because I knew what would be attached to this yes.

I feared that my language and how I would choose to articulate myself would be judged. I feared that those who held tight to that rod of religion would pull apart my words. I feared my testimony wouldn't be enough for the many God desired to reach. I feared those who needed freedom would turn down freedom because they saw my story as just a good turnaround for me and not for themselves. I feared those who might come up against me because I was preaching against something culture is for. Although these fears can seem natural for someone like myself, who has never done this before, I realized that the type of fear that cripples you is not a natural kind of fear. That is a spirit at work.

"For God has not given me a spirit of fear but of power, love, and a sound mind." 2 Timothy 1:7 (NKJV)

God used this process, this assignment, to expose me to me. I could see that these fears had everything to do with me. But I had to keep crawling back on the altar until I died to myself. And I did exactly that; I kept crawling back on the altar until all that resistance and fear of man died. As I had mentioned earlier, I knew that coming forth with this type of testimony, I had to be courageous and that the fear of man could not be a part of my makeup. I had to be bold and undaunting because of how the Lord wanted me to share my story- raw and uncut. I like to say that God has a way of making you ready. He will use the good, bad, and ugly as a training ground. And let me just say this: so many things happened during this time that forced me to be ready.

Those of us who are brave enough to come forward and share our story no matter what could be said or done demonstrate our commitment to obedience. If they talked about Jesus, what would make me, or anyone else, an exception? You will be loved by some but hated by many. See Matthew 10:23

We see a clear paradigm of this very thing throughout the Bible. When Jesus confronted the religious Pharisees and Sadducees, Jesus purposely confronted their hypocrisy because they placed yolks on the people they could not bear themselves. He confronted their unbelief and their pride, and they hated Him for it. So much so that they plotted against Him. We know how badly the apostles and some of the prophets were beaten, ostracized, and martyred. They laid down their life, literally, to follow Jesus. Dying the worst deaths because of their bold faith and bold evangelism to the world.

I think it's fair to say that what I feared pales in comparison to the trials endured by these great pioneers of faith. And even for many believers worldwide who are being persecuted in this way today as we speak. I don't know what persecution will look like in my nation, but I have the freedom to share right now.

There was a time when someone not liking me rubbed me the wrong way. Or even would make me over-obsessive about how I could have sweetened up a declarative truth. But when I read through the word and see how these great pioneers of the faith moved through this, I cannot and will not be apologetic. By the enablement of the Holy Spirit, I will be brave enough to choose obedience over comfort, risk over safety, and God over Carmen.

It is beyond a question that this Kingdom come; thy will be done is not about followers, fame, or clout. In fact, everything that has to do with extending the true Kingdom of God could be considered extreme, unorthodox, and even demonic to those who are lukewarm or just hard-hearted. So, I am willing to look like a fool because He will take the foolish things to confound the wise. See 1 Corinthians 1:27. Fearing the fierceness and heat of the fire is not a good enough excuse to say "No" to obey. Look at the story of Shadrach, Meshach, and Abednego and ask if they bowed because it was too hard.

I am switching gears as I reach the end of this journey with my story. Many times, I thought about how I should land this plane. It always looked a lot like speaking directly to the ones I knew would be able to relate to my story. I thought about those who are still in the same cycles of pain, hurt, and unforgiveness towards themselves and others. I considered those who felt misunderstood, overlooked, and rejected. I also thought about those stuck between transitions. I thought about those far from the Father but close to His heart. I asked the Father about these. The ones I know He has laid His finger on.

As you read this, I pray that your heart is open to embrace a divine visitation from God. That you would make room for Him to come in and wreck your life. I declare that as your heart opens up to Him, your space will become a rendezvous, a meeting place where you can connect with your heavenly Father—the One who took His time to form you ever so intricately with His very hands in your mother's womb. See Jeremiah 1:5

If you have identified yourself in any part of me and want to take a bold step in having a relationship with the One who turned everything around for me. Then this is your personal invitation to encounter the same God I encountered then and the same God that walks with me now—Jesus Christ. In your own words, with no formality, confess that you are a sinner needing a savior. Repent and turn away from your sin, and live for Jesus. Ask Him to come into your heart and possess you fully. Now, may I say welcome to the family, cookie bear!

Let me emphasize on this. God is a personal God. He is not sitting on a throne somewhere in another dimension playing SIMS with your life and waiting for you to screw up to send down fire and brimstone. Quite the contrary, He is patiently waiting for you to run toward Him. He will satisfy your soul in a way that no relationship, addiction, career, money, or anything in this world could ever satisfy you. He can be trusted. Failure and deceit are not in His character. There are no traces of violation in Him. There is no resemblance of the pain you have been through with people in Him. He isn't anything like religion, where having a relationship is burdensome. His yoke is easy, and His burden is light. See Matthew 11:30

Let me inform you that this journey is not all cupcakes and rainbows. This walk is not for the faint of heart; it can and will be challenging, but I can assure you that the beauty will always outweigh the pain. There will be a process, a process that will be hard, a process that will undo everything that you have done. But He's allowing it because He loves you, and because

He loves you, He cannot leave you the same way you came to Him. I want to end with this passage of scripture that defined my story, found in Isaiah 61:1-3 (NKJV)

"1 The Spirit of the Lord God is upon Me, Because the Lord has anointed Me To preach good tidings to the poor; He has sent Me to [a]heal the brokenhearted, To proclaim liberty to the captives, And the opening of the prison to those who are bound; 2 To proclaim the acceptable year of the Lord, And the day of vengeance of our God; To comfort all who mourn, 3 To [b]console those who mourn in Zion, To give them beauty for ashes, The oil of joy for mourning, The garment of praise for the spirit of heaviness; That they may be called trees of righteousness, The planting of the Lord, that He may be glorified."

The name of this chapter is called "The Good News of Salvation." This chapter speaks of a prophecy written by the Prophet Isaiah for the Israelites who went into exile. This prophecy was a message of hope to God's people, a promise of redemption, and a reminder of His love and compassion towards them. This scripture is known as the fulfillment of the ministry of Jesus. For me, this is not just a historical event or a fulfilled prophecy; it is an ongoing fulfillment, as He has done the same for me. He is the anointed one who broke the power of sin over me; He freed me from spiritual and physical impoverishment. He healed the broken parts of my soul. He took everything I saw as irreversible damage in my life and made it a masterpiece. See Ephesians 2:10

He gave me a new name and an identity found in Him. And because of that, I am not who I used to be; I am who He called me to be. He took everything in me that wasn't like Him and gave me everything He is. He gave me a new heart, His heart. His blood blotted out my shame, my guilt, and my sin.

"As far as the east is from the west, so far as he has removed my transgressions from me." Psalms 103:12 (NIV)

He throws them all in the sea of forgetfulness and remembers my sins no more. He is the one who took everything I defined as meaningless and gave it meaning. He is the giver of life. The one who comes to give life and life more abundantly. He is the Great I am, the one who is and is to come, the Alpha, the Omega-The Beginning and The End. He is Elohim God the creator. El Shaddai-The Lord God Almighty. Adonai- my Lord and Master. He is Yahweh. He is Jehovah Jireh, my provider. Jehovah Nissi, my banner. Jehovah Rapha—God, my healer. He is El Roi—The God who sees me. He is my Abba–Father. He is my hiding place, my fortress, and the source of my strength, joy, and peace. He gave me the oil of gladness for mourning, the garment of praise for the spirit of despair. There is no other explanation for what has happened in my life. I would just say that... Its Beauty for Ashes!